MOVEMENT PRINCIPLES &
SMOOTH

BY XIAN GOH

Photography by Charlotte Bull
Cover design by Chris Luk
Interior design by Simon Thompson

ISBN: 978-1-0687993-0-3

In loving memory of my dad
Goh Hwee Poh
who taught me to observe
quietly and live boldly.

CONTENTS

PREFACE

I've been climbing for 18 years, and I've been actively pursuing progress for most of that time. Over the years, I've tried many different training plans but have repeatedly found myself not achieving the result I am looking for: climbing better. On the more successful rounds of training, I felt stronger and I had more time to climb before I ran out of energy. However, I didn't feel like I was getting much better. On the less successful rounds of training, I found myself tired and on the brink of injury (or actually injured). At the worst points, I felt unmotivated from spending more time watching the clock than climbing! It never felt like an effective way of improving.

Luckily, over the years, I've met many inspirational climbers and visited all kinds of amazing crags. By watching and speaking with those who make climbing look easy, I discovered ways of moving that made climbing infinitely easier. By repeatedly throwing myself onto boulders and routes that made no sense to me, I eventually, through pig-headed trial and error, uncovered their secrets and got myself to the top. It was not through training but exposure to technically stimulating environments that I learnt to climb and take tangible steps forward.

And finally, through coaching and trying to coherently explain to other climbers what I had learnt, I started to distil the core principles of good climbing technique. Every coaching session was a test of understanding. I had to adjust my advice to suit each individual's ability, strength, and size. This helped me to distinguish universal principles that apply to everyone from surface details that change from person to person.

As much as I've enjoyed my meandering journey of learning, it seems an incredibly long-winded way to learn a new skill. There appears to be a scarcity of resources about climbing technique, which is surprising, as movement technique is one of the key skills of climbing! This is why I've decided to share what I've learnt.. I hope that you find it useful and that it will expand your enjoyment and understanding of the wonderful world of climbing.

INTRODUCTION

HELLO THERE!

We're about to embark on your **SMOOTH** journey. Before we start, here are a few things that might be helpful.

VOCABULARY

Here are some terms that we will be using to describe movement. I've tried to use language that is as plain as possible, using technical terms only where there are no good alternatives.

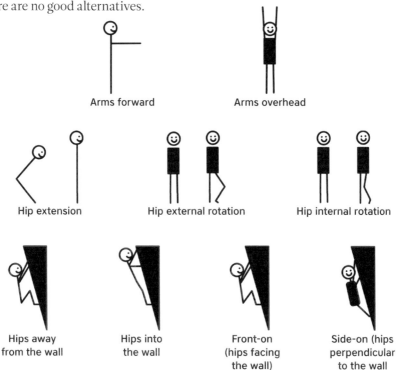

Arms forward   Arms overhead

Hip extension   Hip external rotation   Hip internal rotation

Hips away   Hips into   Front-on   Side-on (hips
from the wall   the wall   (hips facing   perpendicular
                                        the wall)   to the wall

HOW TO USE THIS BOOK

In Part 1, I have outlined the structure through which I view climbing technique. In Parts 2, 3 and 4, I will go into the details of the specific techniques and how to execute them well. In Part 5, I bring all the information together to explain how it all combines to form a cohesive system. I also give some suggestions on how to self-assess your climbing and target specific areas for improvement.

Throughout the book, I have used a combination of photos and illustrations, depending on what I thought would demonstrate the point most effectively. I've included exercises to help you explore and practise each technique.

There are three types of exercises:

1. Explore: These are designed to help you build awareness and understanding through exploration. Be curious, be mindful, and really think about it.
2. Develop: These are designed to help you improve your skill level of each technique. Pay attention to the detail and adjust on each attempt to increase the standard of execution.
3. Practise: These are designed to help you achieve a consistently high standard of execution of each technique through high quality repetitions. Be disciplined and hold yourself to account.

There is more detail in Chapter 15 on how to use these exercises as part of a technique programme. You can find videos for all the drills on my website:

xiangoh.com/smooth.

I have structured the book so it makes the most sense if you read it from front to back. The order also reflects how I would usually build a technique programme for climbers with whom I work. The skills mentioned in a chapter lay the foundation for the skills mentioned in the next chapter. That being said, each chapter focuses on only one topic. This means you can also use it like a textbook, referencing each topic in the order you are most excited about.

Before we dive into the details, let's address the million-dollar question...

Is there a right and wrong way to climb?

One thing I love about climbing is that it is both extremely complex and crystal clear! There are a million ways to move, yet it is always apparent whether each way is right or wrong. This is where I stand:

1. If what you did was enough to complete the climb, then it must be right.
2. If there is another way to complete the climb with less effort, then that way must be better.
3. Right and wrong is determined by success and failure.
4. There are multiple ways to be right, and some ways are superior to others.

Regardless of your current climbing level, I hope you will find this a useful resource to improve your ability and enrich your experiences.

Thank you for picking up this book! I would love to hear from you. If you have any questions or feedback, please get in touch at xiangoh.com.

1

PRINCIPLES AND PATTERNS

1

PAYING ATTENTION TO THE RIGHT THINGS

PRINCIPLES VS. SURFACE DETAILS

Climbing is special because we are constantly doing different things. No two climbs are exactly the same. Climbers too are unique, and often each climber will have a slightly different way of climbing up to the top. Even at the highest level, such as in the World Cup competitions, we see climbers of similar heights solving climbs with different beta. This suggests that there is no single best way but rather multiple equally good ways of climbing.

With so much variation and chaos, how can we know what good technique is? Consistent good performance is based on the ability to create repeating patterns. The first step is being able to distinguish universal principles from surface details. Universal principles are usually about physics and physiology. They are about intersecting the laws of both realms in a synergistic way. Here are some examples:

- Moving your centre of gravity to a position of balance.
- Timing a strong pull at the top of the swing.
- Pushing through your legs in the direction that best weights your foothold.

Most good climbers are executing these principles most of the time. However, how they go about doing it can look very different:

- They could be using a different sequence.
- They could be using different footholds.
- They could be gripping the handholds in different ways.
- One person might flag horizontally and another diagonally.
- One person might move very quickly and another very slowly.

These are surface details. We are all different heights, with different relative limb lengths, and we all have different degrees of strength and flexibility. If two people were executing the same principle, they would be unlikely to end up in exactly the same shape.

In this book, we are going to discuss the principles of climbing technique. It is up to you, the climber, to figure out how to apply it to your unique self.

BODY AWARENESS

Before we go into the details of climbing movement, let's look at the foundational skill that underpins it all: body awareness.

Body awareness refers to the skill of knowing what your body is doing when you are doing it. Ask yourself these questions:

- What shape is my body in?
- Which parts of my body are moving? Which parts are still?
- When did I start moving? When did I stop?
- How did I generate movement? How did I resist movement?
- Where do I feel tension? Where do I feel relaxed?
- Where is my body in space?

It's a remarkably difficult skill to acquire, as most movement is born from the unconscious mind. While it may not be possible to become fully aware of every movement in your body, being mindful of what is going on will go a long way towards helping you:

- recognise what you did on accidental successes
- realise what contributed to past mistakes and correct accordingly
- more reliably climb at the standard you are capable of
- learn from your body's innate wisdom.

Chances are, we've all done some good-quality movement at some point. I'm referring to those days when 'everything just feels right' or when a move we've been working on for ages suddenly feels easy. When we climb well, it feels good. It feels like we're floating and is, for many climbers, the reason we keep coming back for more. Unfortunately, those moments can also feel elusive and hard to recapture.

Consider this scenario:

- Mei is projecting a climb at her local wall.
- Mei starts the climb, carries on to the crux move, and falls off. Mei tries the same climb a few more times, falling off at the same place each time. On her fifth go, she gets to the crux, and the movement suddenly just 'feels right'. She does the move, it feels easy, and she continues to the top.

- Mei is very happy with her climbing efforts. She is not sure what she did differently but is proud of herself for persevering and trying a little harder. Mei moves on to the next climb.

Is this you? If so, you may have to work on your body awareness. Plenty of sends can be made by clocking up enough attempts and having a peppy attitude. However, without good body awareness, this is unlikely to result in significant progress. If we don't know what we did, we cannot replicate success or make changes from failed attempts. If we cannot control our body, we cannot change our movements. If we aren't aware of what's going on, we cannot learn from experience.

The goal for long-term progress is to increase our proportion of good-quality movement. Awareness helps us step out of the cycle of trial and error, and progress forward in a meaningful way.

EXPLORE
MEMORY VS. VIDEO

These exercises will help you build awareness of the more obvious aspects of climbing. Developing your skill here will give you a good foundation for developing awareness of more abstract aspects of climbing, like weight distribution, balance, and potential energy.

VERSION 1: SEQUENCE

1. Set up your phone to film yourself climbing.
2. Do a climb.
3. When you get back down to the ground, take a moment to recall the sequence of moves you did.
4. Check the video to see if your recall was accurate.
5. Repeat as needed until you can accurately recall what you did.

VERSION 2: CRUX MOVES

1. Set up your phone to film yourself on a difficult move that you are not yet able to do.
2. After you fall off, take a moment to recall what position your body was in before you fell off:
   a. Where were your hands?
   b. Where were your feet?
   c. Where were your hips?
3. Check the video to see if your recall was accurate.
4. Use this information to help you to brainstorm ideas for solving this move.
5. Repeat until you can do the move!

THE BIG FIVE

Most climbers, whether watching another or recalling their own attempts, will pay attention to the surface details such as:

- sequence
- what the arm is doing (bent or straight)
- what the feet are doing (which foothold they are on and where exactly the flag was)
- how easy or difficult it looked or felt.

When trying to watch and learn from another climber, these notes are so literal that they are only useful in a 'copy and paste' scenario where you copy like-for-like what the other climber is doing. When trying to analyse your previous attempts, these notes are too obvious, and many climbers run out of ideas about what to try next very quickly.

Try asking yourself these questions instead:

1. Am I stable or am I moving?
2. Where is my weight?
3. Where did I start moving from?
4. Which direction did I move in?
5. Did I apply the right amount of force to arrive at the right position?

These questions bring your attention to the universal principles that apply to all climbing movement – the Big Five:

1. Climbing is made up of two repeating phases: stable and move.
2. Always pay attention to weight distribution.
3. Movement flows from the bottom up.
4. Move in the correct 3D direction.
5. Not too much, not too little, just the right amount.

PRINCIPLE 1:
CLIMBING IS MADE UP OF TWO REPEATING PHASES: STABLE AND MOVE
STABLE AND MOVE

Every climb can be broken down into a series of two repeating phases:

1. Stable
2. Move

The stable phase is where:

- you feel stable
- your centre of gravity is mostly still, but you may be moving your arms, legs, or head

This often coincides with being in a balanced position and/or with holding some tension in the body to create rigidity. We tend to naturally adopt a stable position when we want to pause, shake off, and/or assess our situation.

The move phase is where:
- you are moving
- your centre of gravity is travelling through space

Movement usually arises from being out of balance or as a response to some form of force being applied (such as a push or a pull) or a mix of the two. We tend to generate movement to move towards the next handhold.

THE CLASSIC RHYTHM
Climbing is a mix of both stable and move phases, and the classic rhythm of climbing goes like this:

Stable, move, stable, move, stable, move...

<table>
<tr><td>Stable</td><td>Move</td><td>Stable</td></tr>
<tr><td>Move</td><td>Stable</td><td></td></tr>
</table>

This rhythm is the basis of most climbing. Even up to the highest level of climbing, especially in outdoor climbing, we still see the climbers sending the hardest climbs using this rhythm. Don't just take my word for it, here's an exercise to help you see it for yourself.

EXPLORE:
STABLE–MOVE 'DRUMMING'
This is an exercise in observation and can help you learn more from watching climbing videos.

1. Watch an uncut video of your favourite climber.
2. Tap your left hand on the table when you see a stable phase and your right hand when you spot a move phase.
3. What was the rhythm of their climb?

Now do this exercise while watching a video of yourself climbing. What's your rhythm?

COMMON MISTAKES
Climbers who do not use the classic stable–move rhythm often fall into one of the following categories:

1. Move, move, move, move, fall off

   These climbers are constantly on the move. They do not pause and do not regularly establish stability as they climb. Often the mentality is one of rushing: 'I feel unstable, so I have to get to the next hold before I fall off.' Essentially, the strategy here is trying to outclimb gravity. This is, of course, a short-lived strategy, as it is physically exhausting to be constantly fighting a swing.

2. Stable, stable, stable, stable, stuck

   These climbers are adept at finding balanced stable positions. They present as slow and hesitant, pause frequently, and often find themselves stuck, not knowing how to get to the next handhold. This mentality is often one that over prioritises caution and certainty. The climber enjoys the feeling of stability and is hesitant to leave the comfort of a balanced position. The longer they stay in the stable phase the harder it is to leave. This is because, as they fatigue physically, the movement seems even more uncertain making it even harder to leave the comfort of stability. It's no surprise that this strategy rarely leads to success.

These are, of course, extreme examples to illustrate a point. It's important to recognise whether you have a tendency towards either of these behaviours so that you can course correct accordingly.

OTHER RHYTHMS

Coordination moves – the most recent innovation in movement technique – disrupt the classic rhythm. They often go like this:

Stable, move, move, move, stable...

This is an intelligent hack, as a coordination move is the solution to the section of the climb that is so sparsely featured that there are no stable positions available.

Sometimes we may also choose to bypass the stable phase to create efficiency:

Stable, move, move, stable...

Skilled climbers can do this elegantly, carrying the momentum from one move into the next to maximise efficiency. Nevertheless, they still start and end in a stable position and do not suffer from the negative consequences of rushing.

Speed climbing is the only exception: this is about being in the move phase from start to finish. The best speed climbers carry the momentum through from move to move at the highest level without pausing to establish stability.

Regardless, identifying the stable and move phases is a simple but effective framework to help you understand what is going on.

PRINCIPLE 2:
ALWAYS PAY ATTENTION TO WEIGHT DISTRIBUTION
WHERE IS YOUR WEIGHT?

This is quite an abstract question, so let's clarify it: How many contact points do you have weight on?

Now let's build your understanding step by step. The first step is to count your points of contact:

• Do you have one or two hands in contact with the wall?
• Do you have one or two feet in contact with the wall?

These are easy questions to answer, and many people stop here. That is a mistake.

The next step is very important:

• Of your contact points, how many of them are weighted?

If you pay attention to the sensation of weight, you should be able to tell where it is. Here's a test to check if your spidey senses are accurate: If you can remove a point of contact without displacing your centre of gravity, it is not a weighted point.

The goal is to <u>always</u> be able to tell where your weight is.

When you know where your weight is, you can manipulate it to:

• find balance to be stable
• create a stable platform from which to generate maximum force
• disrupt stability and generate momentum
• shift weight from one contact point to another.

Knowing where your weight is distributed is the basis of understanding climbing technique. It is the language that enables us to think and talk about climbing movement.

EXPLORE
TUNING IN

This is a simple ground-based exercise you can do before climbing to help you tune into where your weight is. This is done with your eyes closed to enhance the other senses. It can also help you become more familiar with making adjustments to body position without visual cues.

1. Stand on the ground with bare feet, both feet at hip width apart.
2. Close your eyes.
3. Lean forward such that your weight is on the front of your feet. Pause.
4. Lean backwards such that your weight is on your heels. Pause.
5. Bring your weight back to the centre so it is evenly distributed across each foot.
6. Lean to the left until all your weight is on your left foot only (your right foot is touching the ground but not weighted).
7. Lean to the right until all your weight is on your right foot only.
8. Bring your weight back to the centre so it is evenly distributed across both feet.
9. Open your eyes.

You can also do something similar on a good set of handholds and footholds if you feel confident to do this on the wall.

THE EIGHT POSITIONS

Identifying the number of weighted points of contact gives us a framework for breaking down climbing movement into distinct groups of techniques. All body positions fall into one of these eight categories.

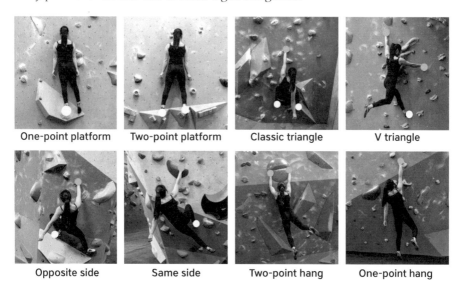

| One-point platform | Two-point platform | Classic triangle | V triangle |

| Opposite side | Same side | Two-point hang | One-point hang |

Each position has its own advantages and disadvantages, and these determine which specific techniques are available. Suddenly, the chaos of infinite variety is made simple.

PRINCIPLE 3:
MOVEMENT FLOWS FROM THE BOTTOM UP
WHERE DID I START MOVING FROM?

Imagine you can press pause, rewind, and watch yourself climbing in slow motion... which body part started moving first?

Of course, we live in the digital age and there is no real need for imagination. You can film yourself climbing and then watch it in slow motion. Ask yourself: What moved first? And then: What followed? These are crucial pieces of information.

In the move phase, movement has to flow from the bottom up – starting from the feet, then flowing up to the lower body and finally to the upper body. This is about doing the right component movements in the right order at the right time. When you achieve this climbing feels easy. It creates synergy, and your entire body is working cohesively towards the same goal. Disregard this and the opposite occurs. All the parts of your body are working in conflict with each other and climbing can feel ridiculously difficult.

This is a huge topic, and we will cover it in more detail in Chapter 8.

EXPLORE
SLO-MO CLIMBING

This exercise is a way of putting a magnifying glass on your climbing movement to help you better understand the component parts and how you tend to climb.

1. Look for a climbing move that is very straightforward for you.
2. First, do it as you normally would.
3. Next, do it as slowly as you can. A good challenge is to count to five while you do a single move.
4. Where did you start moving from? Where did your movement flow to?

PRINCIPLE 4:
MOVE IN THE CORRECT 3D DIRECTION
CONNECT THE DOTS

When we move, we are connecting two stable positions. The correct direction to move in follows the line that connects the start and end positions. While we want to always consider the entire body, it is extremely difficult to keep track of all our limbs and where they are in space. A simple hack is to distil yourself into a single dot and then chart the line of movement from dot to dot.

This dot is your midpoint. The midpoint is just below your belly button and halfway between your lower back and your belly.

Midpoint

This is a useful reference point for a few reasons:

- This is where your centre of gravity would be if you were standing. To find stable positions on the wall, we are often trying to recreate the upright nature of standing, with the centre of gravity being around here.
- It is roughly where your hip joint is and can be used to directly cue the hip action, which is crucial in climbing technique.
- It is roughly where your pelvis is, and your trunk sits on top of your pelvis. The trunk accounts for approximately half our body weight and therefore has a big impact on where our weight falls.[1] It is a less mobile part of the body and often the only way to move this chunk of weight is to move the entire pelvis. In climbing the big challenge is to transport your relatively immobile and heavy trunk.

2D VS. 3D

It is important to remember that we exist in a 3D space. Many climbers make the mistake of thinking only in two dimensions, usually remembering up/down and left/right, and neglecting in/out.

This is likely a consequence of standing behind the climber when we are watching someone else climb. This safety practice, which is followed whether bouldering or rope climbing, has exposed us disproportionately to these two dimensions of movement and made it easy to forget about the third one.

Back View

Side View

[1] Stanley Plagenhoef, F. Gaynor Evans, and Thomas Abdelnour. 1983. 'Anatomical Data for Analyzing Human Motion,' Research Quarterly for Exercise and Sport 54 (2): 169–78. doi:10.1080/02701367.1983.10605290.

Before we move, we should plot a line of movement that can connect the start and finish positions. Thinking about all three dimensions of this line can improve your movement tremendously.

TRAINING YOUR EYE

We have to be quite quick to observe movement – sometimes it is over in the blink of an eye! If you find yourself missing this in real life, use videos to help train your eye. You can start by watching a video in slow motion and then gradually speed it up to real time when you have a better sense of what is going on.

We typically use different techniques to move in different directions (we will look at this in more detail in Chapter 9). Having a good awareness of your direction of travel is essential to executing all the techniques to a high level.

EXPLORE
BACK VIEW VS. SIDE VIEW

This is an exercise to investigate how you are currently thinking about 3D space.

1. Film yourself doing the same climb from two different angles (the back view and the side view).
2. First, watch yourself from the back view. Observe how your midpoint moves.
3. Based on the above, what do you think you will see on the side view?
4. Now, watch yourself from the side view. Is this in line with your expectations?

PRINCIPLE 5:
NOT TOO MUCH, NOT TOO LITTLE, JUST THE RIGHT AMOUNT

Ultimately, climbing is a sport based on precision. You could be set up perfectly in a stable position, initiating from the legs, and shooting decisively in the correct direction but, alas, a fraction too little and you find yourself out of reach. A push too far, and you have to fight the swing to stay on. Jugs are forgiving, but crimps are cruel and slopers are slippery. Like a top patisserie chef, we must be exact to achieve the lightness of a croissant in our movements.

We often use the same techniques to solve easy and difficult climbs. Typically, the more difficult climbs have a higher requirement for precision. There is a need to start and end each move at exactly the right spot in order to be able to stay on poor holds and hold outrageous body positions. A precise climber is able to cut out unnecessary movement, and in so doing, improves both efficiency and effectiveness.

We can achieve precision by adjusting many dials. These are the most important ones to get right:

- Amount of force applied.
- Quality of force applied (e.g., explosive, slow and controlled, relaxed and swinging).
- Plotting the exact line of movement that is required.
- Developing our skill of aiming with the whole body.
- Looking at the right parts of the handholds and footholds.

PRECISE PRACTICE

Precision is a core element of climbing. This is why I would not recommend exaggerating a particular movement or technique in order to learn it. In my opinion, all this does is teach us the wrong things:

- Poor application of the technique.
- Poor judgement of how much force to use, direction of travel, aim, and whether this technique is even appropriate for that climb.

Exaggerating a movement creates a disconnect between our conscious mind and our intuitive sense of movement, and this is deeply problematic.

Practising precision, on the other hand, develops our sense of climbing:

- It teaches us how to apply each technique in the right way for each unique climb.
- It hones our judgement about which technique to use and when. This further develops our route-reading and problem-solving skills.
- It deepens the connection between our conscious mind and our intuitive sense of movement, allowing us to be fully present in our climbing.

As a rule of thumb, I would take any climbing advice that starts with 'always' or 'as much as you can' with a pinch of salt. Climbing is quite a complicated movement practice and is very context dependent, so there are few rules that apply all the time.

EXPLORE
PRECISION TAPPING

This exercise explores how precise you are with your movement.

1. Choose three specific points on the wall to aim for. If climbing indoors, bolt holes could be good targets.
2. Get on the wall and establish a stable position. Move towards each target and aim to tap exactly at each point.
3. Did you hit your targets?

SUMMARY

Pay attention to the principles of climbing technique instead of obsessing over surface details.

Body awareness enables us to understand, repeat, and/or change our movements. Be body aware so that you can improve on your past performance.

THE BIG FIVE:

1. Climbing is made up of two repeating phases: stable and move.
2. Always pay attention to weight distribution.
3. Movement flows from the bottom up.
4. Move in the correct 3D direction.
5. Not too much, not too little, just the right amount.

2
ROUTE READING

MOVEMENT SKILLS AND JUDGEMENT SKILLS

There are two types of skills we must develop to master climbing technique: movement skills and judgement skills.

- Movement skills are about moving well and executing the techniques well.
- Judgement skills are about matching the right technique to the right climb.

Both skills are important for creating the result of smooth and effective climbing. Executing each technique to perfection is useless if we apply it to the wrong climb. Knowing exactly what to do without being able to execute it is equally ineffective.

Route reading and problem solving are judgement skills. We're looking at route reading early on in this book, and we'll explore problem solving nearer the end. This mirrors the climbing journey.

- We start off with route reading to scout out and come up with a tentative plan to solve the climb.
- We give it a good go.
- In the event of an unsuccessful ascent, we continue the process with problem solving.

ROUTE READING

In order to find the right techniques for each climb, we need to start by understanding its specific requirements.

COMMON MISTAKES

Many climbers miss the defining features of the climb and instead obsess over minute details such as:

- the size of handholds and footholds
- whether they are able to plot a left-right-left-right hand sequence
- the texture or friction level of holds.

This is another example of how climbers can get distracted by the surface details rather than paying attention to useful principles.

Many climbers also tend to particularly notice the features that worry them the most. For example, a climber who dislikes crimps is very likely to notice that there are crimps on the climb before spotting any other feature. This can then trigger a stress response. The climber probably feels very resistant to trying this climb, and this can lead to further unhelpful obsession over the small details. If you notice yourself doing this, it is important to be aware of this tendency so that you can break the cycle and start route reading effectively instead.

Observing a climb should be a fairly mundane, systematic process that we repeat in a routine way. The climb is the problem. We are searching for the solution. Start with the big picture and then progressively narrow down to the details. This is the logical order, as the big picture provides the context needed to understand the details.

BIG PICTURE: WALL ANGLES

The first feature to pay attention to is the angle of the wall. Is it a slab? Is it an overhang? Is it a roof? How and where does the profile change?

This may seem obvious, but unfortunately it is commonly overlooked. Many climbers will focus on smaller features of the wall, such as the size and direction of the handhold, before they notice the wall angle. This is a rookie error. Paying attention to your handholds and footholds before the wall angle means you have no context to understand whether these are good or bad holds.

We can broadly group wall angles into four categories:[2]

1. Slab ($<0°$)
2. Slight overhang ($0-40°$)
3. Steep overhang ($40-70°$)
4. Roof ($>70°$)

---

[2] Although face climbing (−5° to 5°) does represent a unique challenge, it is distinctive because it requires a mix of both slab and slight overhang techniques. It's therefore not a standalone category but instead a blend of two categories.

The delineation of these categories is based on the impact of gravity on our body position. A stable body position tends to work with the line of gravity. Although gravity always pulls on us in the same direction (vertically downwards), on different wall angles, the stable position can look completely different.

Slab (<0°)

Slight overhang (0–40°)

Steep overhang (40–70°)

Roof (>70°)

It's also important to look out for large features that stick out a lot. Extremely large features can change the angle of the wall significantly. For example, if there were a car-sized tufa sticking out of a roof, it may create a vertical corner feature. Instead of using roof–climbing techniques, we would need to think about this section of the climb as a vertical corner. Smaller but still significantly sized features can also impact the angle noticeably. For example, a laptop-sized ledge on a vertical face can turn that section of the climb into a slab. Instead of adopting a triangle squatting–down position, we may have to switch to more of an upright position.

EXPLORE:
THE ANGLE IS RIGHT!
How good are you at assessing the wall angle? Gather a few friends and see who is best at this.

1. Before you start each climb, ask everyone: What is the angle of this wall?
2. Let everyone respond before checking.
3. Use your phone to check who got it right!

MEDIUM PICTURE: DENSITY OF FEATURES

After accounting for plus-sized features, we want to pay attention to the medium-sized features. These are features that are big enough for one hand or one foot to be on them. I would start by assessing the density of these medium-sized features. How far apart are they from each other? This tells us whether we need to do big moves or small moves.

If the features are tightly packed and close together, it means:

- the moves involved will be smaller
- given the same difficulty rating, the challenge is more likely going to be in establishing stability
- we're more likely to be able to be in a supported position (more weighted points of contact) to generate movement.

If the features are far apart, it means:

- the moves involved are likely to be bigger
- given the same difficulty rating, the challenge is more likely going to be in generating movement
- we're more likely to be in less supported positions (fewer weighted points of contact), which might make it more challenging to generate movement.

Specifically, it is most useful to measure the size of the move relative to your own body length. This will provide useful information to help you decide what techniques to use on each movement.

Here's a size chart you can use:

Size 1: The next handhold is within reach with all three contact points remaining in their initial places.

Size 2: To reach the next handhold, one foot must leave a foothold. This category includes reaches up to one body length.

Size 3: To reach the next handhold, both feet must leave the footholds. The lower hand remains on the initial handhold.

Size 4: To reach the next handhold, all four points must leave the initial handholds and footholds.

The size chart can be used in conjunction with the well-established framework of 'static/dynamic'. To do a move statically is to establish stability at the end of the move phase on the initial handholds and footholds. To do a move dynamically is to establish stability at the end of the move phase on the next set of handholds and footholds. We can choose to do Size 1 moves statically or dynamically. We can do some Size 2 moves statically, and all of them dynamically. We can only do Size 3 and Size 4 moves dynamically.

The size chart describes the problem – what is the distance between the handholds relative to my body length? 'Static/dynamic' describes the solution – how am I going to create stability at the end of the move phase? These frameworks help to clarify thinking, making route reading and problem solving more systematic and effective.

Using this size chart requires you to have an accurate understanding of your body length. Here is an exercise you can do to test and refine this.

EXPLORE
WHAT CAN I REACH?
This exercise is about developing an accurate sense of your body length.

VERSION 1: HOW WIDE CAN I GO?
1. Pick a handhold at approximately shoulder height.
2. Step back from the wall and estimate how far you will be able to reach at full arm span. Pick either a specific point or climbing hold as a marker.
3. Step forward to the wall and measure this distance against your arm span.
4. How accurately did you assess yourself?
5. Repeat as needed with the feedback obtained to improve accuracy.

VERSION 2: HOW HIGH CAN I REACH?
As above, but use a foothold and measure yourself vertically with straight legs and a straight arm overhead.

SMALL DETAILS: HANDHOLDS AND FOOTHOLDS
Now it is finally time to pay attention to the specifics of each handhold and foothold. Look closely at the details, such as the hold profile, direction, texture. These provide important clues as to how we should position our body, and help us assess how difficult we are likely to find these movements. We will go into these in more detail in the respective chapters on footwork (Chapter 6) and gripwork (Chapter 7).

SUMMARY

There are two types of skills related to technique:
- Movement skills
- Judgement skills

Route reading and problem solving are judgement skills.

Route reading should be a mundane, systematic process that we repeat in a routine way.
- Step 1: Big picture: What is the wall angle?
- Step 2: Medium picture: What is the density of the holds?
- Step 3: Small details: What do the handholds and footholds look like?

3

FINALLY, A FRAMEWORK!

A FRAMEWORK FOR CLIMBING TECHNIQUE

One of the problems we have in the climbing world is the lack of a comprehensive framework to understand and think about all the moves we do. The only established framework we have is the binary of 'static/dynamic', which surely is not enough! In my view, this severely limits our ability to understand climbing techniques. This is my proposed solution.

In the previous chapters, I described the factors that I consider to be the pillars of climbing movement. Put together, they form a framework that we can use to categorise and organise all climbing movement:

Movement topic	Breakdown	Techniques
Rhythm	1. Stable 2. Move	• Having distinct phases • Classic stable–move rhythm • Non-classical rhythms
Body position	1. One-point platform 2. Two-point platform 3. Classic triangle 4. V triangle 5. Opposite side 6. Same side 7. Two-point hang 8. One-point hang	• Rest position • Base position • End position
Kinetic sequence	Set the feet → lower body action → upper body action	• Movement flows from the bottom up
Direction of travel	Three dimensions: up/down, left/right, in/out	• Stand up/step up • Rockover • Twist • Hip extension • Downclimb

Wall angle	1. Slab 2. Slight overhang 3. Steep overhang 4. Roof	Adjust body position accordingly
Size of move	1. Size 1: The next handhold is within reach with all three contact points remaining in their initial places. 2. Size 2: To reach the next handhold, one foot must leave a foothold. This category includes reaches up to one body length. 3. Size 3: To reach the next handhold, both feet must leave the footholds. The lower hand remains on the initial handhold. 4. Size 4: To reach the next handhold, all four points must leave the initial handholds and footholds.	Static moves: 1. Small reach move Dynamic moves: 1. Full extension move 2. Cut loose move 3. Dyno
Gripwork and footwork	Size, profile, and direction of holds	• Pivot point • Edging • Foot swaps • Side pull • Undercut • Sloper • Gaston • Crimp • Pinch • etc.

SCOPE OF THIS BOOK

I would love to cover all the topics listed above, but in the interest of completing this book, I have chosen to focus on what I consider to be the foundational techniques:

- Having distinct stable and move phases
- One-point platform, two-point platform, classic triangle, and V triangle
- Gripwork and footwork
- Kinetic chain
- All directions of travel
- Slab and slight overhang
- Size 1 and Size 2 moves

Understanding the principles covered in this book is essential to understanding the more advanced techniques. Watch this space for Volume 2!

2

STABLE PHASE

4

THE BREAD-AND-BUTTER ANGLE

FROM 0° TO 40°

Let's begin with the most ubiquitous wall angle: between 0 to 40° overhanging. This category of wall angle is the 'bread-and-butter angle' because it is what most people are climbing most of the time. This is an important topic to understand well as you will be climbing on these wall angles frequently.

WHAT IS MY BODY DOING?

The basic features of the stable position on this angle are:

- straight arms in an overhead position
- legs in a squat position
- general posture ranges from upright to slightly inverted (your head starts to sit behind your hips) – the steeper the overhang, the more inversion occurs.

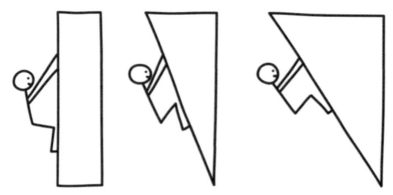

This position works with both the line of gravity and the comfort of the body. The work distribution is aligned with our physiology, with the stronger lower body doing the lion's share of the stabilising work.

BASE POSITION VS. REST POSITION

To transition smoothly between the stable and move phases, we have to distinguish between two types of stable position:

1. Rest position
2. Base position

The rest position is fairly self-explanatory: it's where you take a break and try to recover a little before continuing climbing. As a rule of thumb, you want to spend the least amount of energy here so that you have a chance of recovering! This may be most energy efficient for rest, but it's unlikely that the best position for resting is also a good position for moving off from.

This is why we also have the base position. The base position has a different function. It serves as a kind of base camp or headquarters. This is the position you visit regularly between each move phase but do not stay in for very long. In fact, we often move off almost immediately after re-establishing stability. A good base position supports both the stable and move phases of climbing. It is simultaneously:

• a stable position where we can take a momentary pause
• a strong position where we can generate force and movement.

In short, we are both stable and ready to move. Here, being stable is useful precisely because it will make moving off easier. There is a well-known saying: You can't fire a cannon from a canoe. In contrast with the rest position, it is <u>not</u> the most energy-efficient position to be in, as we will hold a bit more tension so that we are ready to move.

Rest position   Base position

	Rest position	Base position
Are you stable?	Yes	Yes
Are you in the most energy-efficient position to pause and shake off?	Yes	No
Are you ready to move?	No	Yes

Having a clear distinction between these two positions is the key to a smooth execution of the classic stable-move rhythm.

BASE POSITION

The base position is where we are both stable and ready to move.

LOWER BODY: PASSIVE SIT VS. ACTIVE SQUAT

Passive sit

Active squat

If you start in a good position, everything that follows is easier. We want to be in an active squat rather than sinking down in a passive, almost-collapsed sitting position. If we sink too deep into a passive-sit position, usually one of these two events will occur:

- We end up in a very deep squatting position, which is at the end range of our hip, knee, and ankle joint flexibility. This not only has a higher flexibility requirement, but we also need to exert more strength to stand up from there. The result is usually an excessive use of upper body strength.
- Our hips start to fall below our feet, unweighting the footholds, leading to a general feeling of instability or potentially a foot slip. This can lead to unnecessary tensing of the upper body to establish stability or general feelings of stress and increased fear of falling.

How deep to squat is a bit of an art. We want to strike the balance between:

- squatting down low enough such that it is comfortable
- not being so deep into the squat that it becomes difficult to push off and stand up from.

Usually, this means the following elements are in place:

- The hips sit above the feet to maintain some semblance of an upright posture and avoid the problems of inversion.
- The backs of your thighs and your calves are not pressed up against each other.
- You should feel strong and able to push off from your legs to stand up.
- The toes are engaged and pushing down on the foothold.

UPPER BODY: PASSIVE HANG VS. ACTIVE HANG

Passive hang

Active hang

The same principle applies to a hang – we don't want to be in a completely relaxed passive hang. Being too relaxed leads to greater instability and an inability to generate a pull or push. Ask yourself: Is it easier to do a pull up from a slightly higher more engaged position or from a low passive hang? Starting from a passive hang usually leads to excessive use of swinging or feeling stuck.

You want to start your movement from a slightly active position, with some tension supporting your shoulder. When deciding how much to exert, we want to strike the balance between:

- there being enough tension to create stability but not so much as to become rigid
- being ready to pull but not overly tense
- exerting only a little but not so little as to lose stability and readiness to pull.

If you can achieve all three points, then you will have achieved your perfect base position. This is most likely a combination of an active squat in the lower body and an active hang in the shoulder. They should be mutually supporting so that neither lower body nor upper body is solely having to support your entire body weight. The active squat in the lower body is doing a greater proportion of work. However, the value of the upper body supporting the lower body should not be understated. This is especially important as you progress onto harder climbs where the footholds become both scarce and worse.

We might find ourselves in a passive-hang position at the end of a full reach move, where we had to reach to our absolute maximum span, or when we are in the rest position. In these cases, we simply transition from a passive to active hang before moving off.

EXPLORE
PASSIVE VS. ACTIVE
This exercise is about developing your sense of how it feels to be in an active or passive position. We cannot watch ourselves climbing while we are doing it. Therefore, it's more important to know how it feels than how it looks.

Try out each of the following positions:

1. Passive sit
2. Active squat
3. Passive hang
4. Active hang
5. Rest position
6. Base position

BODY SPACING

Another factor that is crucial to whether you have a good base position is body spacing. This refers to how bunched up or stretched out you are. Ideally, we are aiming for a comfortable spacing where:

- our arms are somewhere between fully overhead and directly forward
- our hips sit above the feet
- there is a comfortable amount of bend at the knees.

Worse   Better   Worse

The first skill is to spot the better position where it is available. And the second skill is to learn how to make do with a suboptimal position when it is not available.

EXPLORE
BODY SPACING EXERCISE

This exercise is about developing your sense of body spacing.

1. Find a reasonably hold-dense wall.
2. Pick a starting handhold and a finishing handhold. We are going to move between these two handholds from different footholds.
3. Start with the footholds you would instinctively choose to use. From here, move to the finishing handhold.
4. Return to the starting handhold and use another set of footholds that are 6 inches above the original set. Move to the finishing handhold.
5. Carry on testing out different footholds, moving upwards 6 inches at a time until you are no longer able to do the move.
6. Now use a set of footholds 6 inches below the original set.
7. Carry on testing out different footholds, moving downwards 6 inches at a time until you can no longer do the move.
8. From which set of footholds did the move feel the easiest?

REST POSITION

When you are resting, feel free to adopt passive hang and sit postures if they feel stable. Ultimately, there is a minimum amount of exertion we need to make to stay on the wall, but here we can be more passive in our posture, as there is no requirement to move off directly from this position.

In addition to the body position, these factors impact how well you recover on the wall:

1. Breathing

   First and foremost, remember to breathe! This can be tricky while climbing, but we can reset and catch our breath at the rest position. As a rule of thumb, it helps to stay in your rest position until you regain a regular breath pattern.

2. Relax the body

   Hold just enough tension to maintain stability, and let the rest go. Watch out for excess tension in the face and shoulders, as this is where many people tense up when they feel stressed. Holding too much tension in the shoulders can impact stability, as it can have the effect of de-weighting your foothold, resulting in a more precarious position, which is less useful for recovery.

3. Shake off one arm at a time

   This promotes blood flow and helps clear the feeling of pump in your forearms.

And, of course, don't forget to transition from a passive rest position to an active base position before moving off again.

WEIGHT DISTRIBUTION

Now that we've established the basic form of the stable positions, let's look at weight distribution.

THE PROBLEM WITH BEING A SQUARE

Distributing our weight equally across all four points of contact can create a very stable position. It seems so logical – we're sharing the load equally across the whole body! Unfortunately, this way of thinking shows a lack of forward planning. If we were to remove one contact point, for example, by taking a hand off to reach towards the next handhold, this would immediately result in a swing pulling you away from the wall. In this situation, most climbers would either hold on harder to keep themselves on the wall or fall off. Over time, the climber may learn to pre-empt the swing by always going for moves quickly and powerfully to minimise the time spent without four points on. This can work but is extremely energy inefficient.

1 Weight evenly distributed over four contact points

2 When I remove one contact point...

3 It leads to a big swing

4 And could result in a fall!

BE A TRIANGLE

The solution is simple: be a triangle. Distribute weight over three points, keeping one point free to move towards the next hold.

Square

Triangle

The triangle is a stable position that leaves one limb free to reach towards the next hold. There is also the added bonus that with only three points on, we tend to be less stretched out. We can bend each joint more, meaning we also have more potential for movement.

This is the repeating pattern that we see in climbing even up to the highest levels.

Classic triangle

Mid-move

New classic triangle

BUT I NEED BOTH HANDHOLDS TO STAY ON!

No worries, I completely understand. Yes, it is easier to hold on to two handholds than one. Consider the triangle as more of a conceptual guideline for weight distribution than a literal one. As long as your weight is primarily distributed over three rather than four points, this should allow you the same benefits while still holding on to both handholds.

Weight distributed over four points   Weight distributed over three points

The converse can happen as well – climbers may have three points of contact while distributing the weight primarily only over two points.

Weight distributed over two points   Weight distributed over three points

This is not recommended, as it is a physically much more demanding position than the triangle. It can feel stable, but often, climbers feel stuck and unable to generate movement in this position.

The 'triangle concept' is not about having only three points of contact but rather is a principle about weight distribution. Paying attention to your sense of weight is key step to fully understanding and applying this principle.

EXPLORE
TRIANGLE DRINKING GAME
This exercise is about developing your observation skills and pattern recognition.

1. Look up an uncut video of your favourite climber.
2. Drink (or score a point) every time they form a triangle.

DEVELOP
FIND YOUR TRIANGLE
This exercise trains you to regularly form triangles.

VERSION 1: FOLLOW THE SET CLIMBS

1. Pick a relatively easy boulder problem or route.
2. As you climb up, pause on each handhold in a triangle shape.
   a. If you find a good position, you should be able to take off one hand without destabilising the rest of your body.
   b. A good rule of thumb is to look for a foothold on either side of your handhold.
3. Repeat the same climb, this time climbing it at your natural pace, making sure to visit the same triangle positions you found previously.

VERSION 2: RAINBOW FEET
Do the exercise above but allow yourself to use any footholds available (including those of a different colour) to practise choosing the best foothold. This is a useful exercise for climbers who want to improve their outdoor climbing, where there are no fixed colours to guide your choices.

DEVELOP
EQUALISING ACROSS THREE POINTS
This exercise trains you to distribute weight over three points even in positions where it may not feel natural to do so.

1. Find a very hold-dense wall for this exercise.
2. Pick two good footholds. We want to focus on your understanding of positional complexity, so stick to large footholds to avoid adding too many other factors into the mix.
3. Keeping your feet on these two footholds, move from handhold to handhold, each time pausing to form a stable triangle where you can take the other hand off and stay still.
4. Challenge yourself to use increasingly outrageous handholds.

SUMMARY

Here are the key points for finding your stable positions on a slight overhang (0–40°):

- Be clear on whether you are trying to use a base position or a rest position.
- Use more active stances for the base position; this will facilitate movement.
- Use more passive stances for rest; this is less effortful.
- Consider your body spacing – are your feet too high or too low?
- Distribute your weight into a triangle.

5

SLABS ARE SPECIAL

SLABS ARE ~~SPECIAL~~ SCARY

It's okay, I know: slabs are scary. There's often nothing to hold on to... and nothing to stand on either! Don't worry – you're not alone in feeling this way. A slab is a wall that is off-vertical in the same direction a staircase is. Slabs are different from overhangs because the physics is different, and so we must position ourselves and generate movement differently.

In this chapter, we will explore how you can adjust your body positioning on slabs to find balance and reduce tension. I've learnt how to find moments of calm after many years of teetering, and I hope that one day you will too.

WEIGHT DISTRIBUTION
DON'T FORM A TRIANGLE, FORM A PLATFORM

To form a triangle, you have to hold on with one of your hands. This creates a problem, because on most slab climbs, the handholds are tiny. When we form a triangle, equalising over three points of contact, we put too much weight on

Triangle

Platform

these terrible handholds. This usually results in us letting go (it's too painful!), feeling stuck, or generally having an unpleasant time.

Luckily, the reason why the handholds are tiny is that you don't need them! The platform position simulates standing upright on the ground. This works because climbing a slab is, from a physics perspective, the same as climbing a staircase. Everything that works on the ground works on the slab, except there is a much smaller range to stay in balance and there are much smaller footholds to push off from.

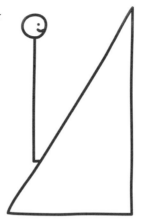

Where a platform is not possible, you can also stand single-legged in pretty much the same position.

Two-point platform   One-point platform

The platform positions are viable with either a straight-leg or a bent-leg. This is similar to how we can stay in balance on the ground with a straight or bent leg.

Bent-leg
two-point
platform

Both the two-point platform and one-point base are stable positions that can be used as a:

- base position
- rest position
- end position

When the knees are bent, we are both stable and ready to move. This fulfils both criteria of the base position.

When the knees are straight, it is usually a more stable position that requires less leg strength. Often, there is the option to take your hands off completely (or hold on only very lightly). The straight-leg platform is usually used as the rest position or end position. Skilful climbers can be almost as relaxed standing on a slab as they are standing on the ground.

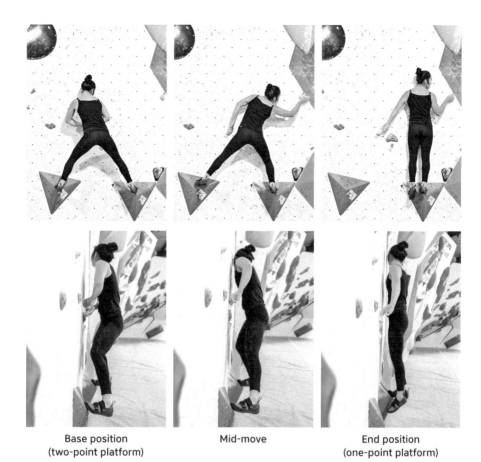

Base position
(two-point platform)

Mid-move

End position
(one-point platform)

EXPLORE
FIND YOUR PLATFORM

This exercise is about finding balanced platform positions on a slab. It can also serve as a self-assessment to see how skilful you are at balancing.

1. Find a slab. The less steep it is, the easier this exercise will be.
2. Find your platform by distributing weight primarily over your feet.
3. Are you able to take your hands off the handholds?

DEVELOP
NO-HANDED PAUSING

This exercise is about identifying and getting comfortable with the balanced platform position in a variety of different positions.

1. Use a slab climb that you find reasonably easy.
2. Pause regularly in no-handed positions as you climb up it.

Many climbers think of the cue 'lean into the wall' when they consider slab positioning. This will help if you are starting out too far from the wall. Unfortunately, if this is not the case, it can lead to a very tense and tentatively balanced position that is easily disrupted.

Pushing your hips too far forward can push you off balance. To compensate, many of us will intuitively start to lean backwards by curving our backs to re-establish balance. While you are technically in balance in this position and can stand still and take your hands off, your entire body is tense and rigid. It then becomes almost impossible to move or, in some cases, even take a breath!

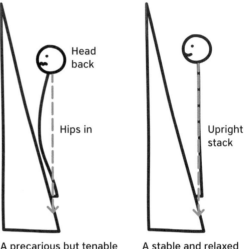

A precarious but tenable balanced position

A stable and relaxed balanced position

DEVELOP
PLATFORM POSITION DANCE OFF

This is about developing the ability to move and stay balanced at the same time.

1. Find a slab. The less steep it is, the easier this exercise will be.
2. Organise your weight to form a no-handed platform position.
3. Can you...
   a. move your head
   b. move your hands
   c. wave your arms in the air like you don't care?
4. Challenge a friend and see who can move the most without falling off.

BUT I NEED MY HANDS TO STAY ON THE WALL!

Again, I understand. Of course, it is easier if you hold on with your hands as well. As long as the weight is distributed primarily over your platform, it is not a problem to keep your hands on the handholds. The role of your arms on the slab is to be more of an important accessory than an equal partner to your legs. They help you stay in balance and improve your stability.

For example, standing on one leg on your tiptoes is quite challenging, so you may only be able to do this for a few seconds. If you place one finger on a wall, this reduces the balance challenge and improves stability significantly. Now you might be able to stay in this position for a minute. The single finger is doing important work, but it certainly is not the star player. It is there to enable your legs to do what they can do for longer and more easily.

IMPROVE YOUR BALANCE

Many climbers who find it difficult to find this balanced platform position and tend to grip with their hands very tightly. If this is you, here are some exercises you can do to improve and connect with your intuitive sense of balance.

DEVELOP
STANDING ON ONE LEG

These ground-based exercises can help you to improve your balance in general.

In order of increasing difficulty:

1. On the ground, stand on one leg and find your balance.
   Hold for 30 seconds to 1 minute.
2. As above, with your eyes closed.
3. As above, waving your arms around.
4. As above, moving your legs around.

DEVELOP
SINGLE-LEG HIGH FOOT

This exercise is about improving your balance on the wall.

1. On a slab, find a balanced one-point platform position.
2. Lift your free leg without destabilising your balance and tap a nearby foothold.
3. Lift the same leg again and tap another nearby foothold.
4. Repeat, exploring how far you can reach without losing balance.

SUMMARY

Here are the key points to remember when you are on a slab:

- Form a platform, not a triangle.
- Stand upright.
- Your lower body is the star of this show.
- Connect with your intuitive sense of balance.

6

FEET FIRST

PUT YOUR BEST FOOT FORWARD

Footwork is the bedrock of good climbing technique. Everything we've learnt about stable body positions so far is reliant on your foot being a stable and reliable point of contact.

If your feet are stable, your lower body is in play. If your feet are not stable, even if they stay on the footholds, the rest of your body has to do a lot of stabilising work, meaning you cannot move them freely. This chapter is about how to step so that your feet are stable.

WHAT ARE WE TRYING TO ACHIEVE?

There are two goals of good footwork:
- Being stable enough to create a platform to push off from.
- Allowing movement so that we can access most of our hip function.

There are three things we have to do to achieve these goals:
- Read the foothold well.
- Place the foot well.
- Connect the foot and the foothold.

READING THE FOOTHOLD

Not all footholds are made equal – a skilled climber is able to identify the best part of the foothold as quickly as a student can spot beer on discount.

These are the five key qualities we are looking out for:

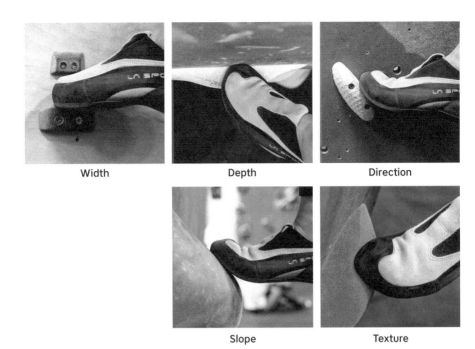

Width	Depth	Direction
Slope	Texture	

The foothold will provide more support if it is:

- wider
- deeper
- horizontal
- in-cut
- rougher.

These are the adjustments we can make to improve foot grip:

Quality	Adjustments
Narrow	Be mindful not to pivot off it.
Shallow	Use edges instead of pivot point.
Vertical	More consciously press against it before standing up on it.
Sloped	Place foot on in a smearing way (more details below).
Smooth/polished	Push down more.

Learning to identify the qualities of your foothold is important because it:

- informs how and on precisely which part of the foothold to place our foot
- helps us to decide between foothold options. This is especially relevant when climbing outdoors, where there is an overwhelming amount of choice
- helps us to determine how supportive a foothold can be, which is crucial information for route reading and problem solving.

How straightforward this will be may depend on how sensitive you are to visual factors such as light, shadow, and form. Here's a quick exercise to test your judgement.

DEVELOP:
EYES VS. HANDS VS. FEET

This exercise explores and develops the connection between your visual and tactile judgement.

1. Pick a foothold at random.
2. Pick out, just by looking, the best part of the foothold.
3. Use your hand to touch the foothold and determine where you would choose to hold it if it were your handhold. Many people find it easier to correctly identify the best part of the foothold via the sense of touch in their hands. Does your hand agree with your eye's judgement?
4. Your feet are the judge. Step on all the identified spots to determine which is in fact the best. The best part of the foothold is the one that feels the most stable when you stand on it.
5. Repeat on different footholds until your eyes and your feet agree.

Once you can spot the best part of the foothold, the next step is to convert this to habit. The goal is to assess your footholds accurately 100% of the time. Yes, that means every single time you lay eyes on a foothold. We don't want this to interfere with the optimal pacing of climbing, which means that we need to practise this until we can do it in a split second.

PLACING THE FOOT

In order for our foot to support our climbing, we need it to stay on the foothold throughout the *entire move phase*. We want this point of contact to be weighted and secure from when the foot is flat all the way to the top of the tiptoe.

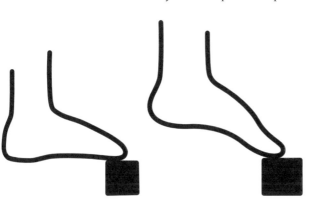

We also want it to be weighted and secure as we rotate. Mechanically, our toes and knees should point in the same direction. If we do any rotation, the feet must pivot.

If we do not place our foot well, then one of these three events is likely to happen:
- We will feel stuck in one position as we intuitively sense that any movement will destabilise us.
- A foot slip – if we rotate anyway, this may lead to the foot pivoting off the foothold.
- Injury – if we persist with rotation while still pressing the foot in a fixed position, this can result in a lot of torque at the knee or ankle and may lead to injury.

PIVOT POINT

This is why, most of the time, we want to step on the pivot point. Stepping on the pivot point allows us to both tiptoe and rotate without slipping off.

Stepping on the pivot point

Make sure the pivot point is in contact with the best part of the foothold and then turn your foot to get as much of the edges of your foot on the foothold as possible. This will allow you to prioritise the pivot function while still gaining some additional support.

EXPLORE
FIND YOUR PIVOT POINT

The easiest way to aim accurately with your pivot point is to be able to both see it and feel it.

1. Stand on the ground with your climbing shoes on.
2. Tiptoe, and hold yourself in balance at the top of the tiptoe.
3. Notice how all your weight comes together to a single point. That is your pivot point.
4. Now look down and learn to recognise what standing on your pivot point looks like from a bird's eye view.

STEP AND TIPTOE

In order to be stable on the foothold, we also need to tense our foot muscles a little to create rigidity. The goal is to create a horizontal platform from which the rest of the foot can push off. It is easy to miss this step because the action is not visible – it is an extremely subtle movement, and the entire action is hidden inside the shoe! You can spot this adjustment by paying attention to the angle between the front of the foot and the foothold.

This an example of insufficient foot tension being used when the foot is placed:

The front of the foot is tending to a vertical angle.

This results in a foot slip as the climber transfers weight onto the right foot.

This is an example of sufficient foot tension being used when the foot is placed:

The front of the foot is tending to a horizontal angle.

The foot stays secure after weight is transferred to the right foot.

If we have an in-cut foothold, then we simply mimic the slope with an angled platform instead of a horizontal platform.

Digging in on an in-cut foothold

EXPLORE:
FIND YOUR FOOT CRIMP

This exercise is about exploring how to use your foot muscles to create rigidity.

1. With bare feet, scrunch up your feet in a half crimp shape.
2. Hold for 5–10 seconds.

MY FEET HURT >.<

It is not uncommon for people to find standing on the pivot point painful or extremely uncomfortable. This could be exacerbated by an ill-fitting shoe. Ideally, the pivot point should be on the base of the big toe. If the pivot point is on your toenail, this is a sign that your shoes may be too small for you. If you are experiencing a great strain on your muscles on the base of your feet, this could be a sign that:

- your shoes are too loose-fitting and therefore not supporting your foot well
- your shoes are too soft for what you are trying to climb
- you are not creating enough tension in your foot
- you are using a foothold that is too small for your current level of foot strength.

Unfortunately, the presence of mild discomfort is a fairly standard hallmark of climbing. This does not mean that you should push yourself into pain regularly. If you experience pain when trying to pivot, I suggest that you try making adjustments, such as changing shoes or using bigger footholds. Ideally, we practise at a level of mild discomfort rather than pain (it is unlikely we can ever achieve comfort). This is more likely to lead to good results as:

- you are more likely to have a positive experience and therefore actually do the practice
- it creates better conditions for reducing sensitivity in your feet in the long term.

Over time, your strength and skill will improve such that you can do more and more spectacular things without increasing your level of discomfort.

PIVOT

Stepping on the pivot point...   allows us to pivot smoothly!

Even though it sounds simple, pivoting can be a surprisingly challenging skill. To pivot well, we need to concentrate all the pressure onto a single point, which acts as the pivot point. This means that this single point will stay at the same location throughout the entire movement. It can help to imagine your big toe as a pin. A common mistake is to place the foot well initially but exert pressure along the ball of the foot. This will cause your foot to wiggle out of place, leading to the dreaded foot slip.

DEVELOP
PIN, TIPTOE, AND PIVOT
This exercise is designed to help you identify exactly where the pivot point is on your shoe, which is also where you have to exert pressure.

1. Pick a foothold smaller than your palm.
2. Holding on to your shoe with your hands, simulate a step, tiptoe, and pivot.
3. Use this to work though the following details:
4. Precisely where the pivot point of your shoe is.
5. The range through which you can pivot on this particular foothold without losing the pivot point.
6. Now try to replicate it exactly with your foot in the shoe – step on, tiptoe, and pivot on the foothold:
7. Step onto the foothold.
8. Tiptoe up and down. Look down to see if your pivot point has moved to determine the quality of your attempt.
9. Pivot round and back. Look down to see if your pivot point has moved to determine the quality of your attempt.

PRACTISE
STAND AND PIVOT
Now that you can pivot well, it's time to put in the mileage to turn it into a habit!

1. You can use a slab, vertical, or slightly overhanging wall.
2. Step and pivot on every move.
3. Repeat the entire climb if there were any poor-quality placements en route.

OUTSIDE
EDGE

INSIDE EDGE

Stepping on the inside edge

Stepping on the outside edge

There is one downside to stepping on the pivot point: it is not as supportive as standing on your edges. The edges of your climbing shoe tend to be stiffer and therefore naturally form a more stable platform to push off from. However, using edges can limit the degree to which we can rotate in our hip and generally reduces movement options in the lower torso. This can result in the feeling of being stuck or can lead to foot slips.

Nevertheless, your edges can be very useful when:
- using very thin or microscopic footholds (what constitutes small is, of course, relative to each individual)
- climbing on wall angles where we need to put a lot of weight through our feet such as slabs and vertical faces.

We simply need to be mindful not to rotate our hips (too much) in this situation to avoid foot slips.

EXPLORE
THE EDGE OF EDGES

This exploration is about developing body awareness. We are exploring the conditions of a foot slip, so you should be prepared for an uncontrolled fall. Use a part of the wall you are happy to fall off from.

VERSION 1: INSIDE EDGE

Standing on your inside edge naturally puts your hip into more of an externally rotated position, and so it will have an impact on how the rest of your body moves.

1. Standing on your inside edge on a flat foothold (neither in-cut nor slopy), test the extent to which you can:
   a. tiptoe
   b. pivot
   c. lift the other leg up
   d. straighten up to full extension.

VERSION 2: OUTSIDE EDGE

Standing on your outer edge naturally places your hips perpendicular to the wall. This will change your options for balance and stability.

1. Standing on your outside edge on a flat foothold, test the extent to which you can:
   a. tiptoe
   b. pivot
   c. lift the other leg up
   d. straighten up to full extension.

PIVOT POINT VS. EDGES

There are pros and cons to using either the pivot point or the edges:

	Pivot point	Edges
Pros	Allows more hip movement	More stable
Cons	Less stable	Restricted hip movement

Ideally, a climber would be proficient in both options and choose the best option for each situation.

EXPLORE

EDGES VS. PIVOTS

This exploration is to help you decide when to use which stepping method. The best way to understand the trade-off is to compare directly.

1. Use a climb that is relatively straightforward for you.
2. Climb it once using only your pivot points.
3. Climb it again using only your edges.
4. Compare and contrast: Which stepping method was better for which move?
5. Repeat the climb one last time, using what you consider to be the best combination of pivot points and edges.

Repeat this exploration on different styles of climbs to expand your understanding.

SMEARS

When smearing on a negative slope, we need to step differently. The placement starts at the pivot point but continues along the 'smear radius'.

Smearing along the smear radius

How to smear:

| Place foot following the grain of the slope | Lift heel up | This pushes pressure onto the front of the foot | Friction between the two surfaces create grip |

In contrast to the pivot point technique, where all the pressure culminates in one point, for smears, we are aiming for even pressure across the front of the foot up to the ball of the foot.

To maintain grip when moving, we have to be mindful not to tiptoe too far.

Too much tiptoe   The right amount

Some climbers are overly conscientious about following the advice to 'keep your heels down'. This can lead to overcompensating, lowering the heels so far that the calf is in a stretched position. Holding your calf at full stretch means that:

- you are less able to make tiny adjustments to stabilise as your body moves, making your position more tenuous.
- the entire leg is rigid, making any form of movement difficult and awkward.

The other consequence of lowering the heels too far is that your centre of gravity can move from being over the front of the foot, to being over your heels. This means that weight is being shifted away from the contact point, and can lead to:

- a foot slip
- leaning the hips very close to the wall to correct the balance point, resulting in rigidity across the entire torso.

Remember, more is not always more. What we're aiming for is just the right amount (Principle 5)!

Heels too low

The right amount

EXPLORE
THE LIMIT OF SMEARS

This exercise helps you develop an objective understanding of what degree of movement is acceptable on each smear. We are exploring the conditions of a foot slip, so you should be prepared for an uncontrolled fall. Use a part of the wall you are happy to fall off from. Be prepared to push yourself away from the wall if you are using a slab.

1. Start by standing on a smear in the way that you think is best.
2. Tiptoe as far as you can. You can either go up to the point where it feels sketchy or, if you are feeling brave, to the point where your foot slips.
3. Drop your heels as low as you can. Again, you can go up to the point where it feels sketchy or, if you are feeling brave, to the point where your foot slips.
4. Now that you know what the upper and lower limits of the smear are, bounce on your feet within the acceptable zone to get used to allowing some movement on the smear.
5. Repeat on different footholds with a similar profile.

CONNECTING THE FOOT AND FOOTHOLD

The final piece of the puzzle is the story of the foot and foothold. How do we get them to stay together through all the trials and tribulations of an entire climb?!

'THE FLOATING FOOT'

When I first started coaching, I would focus a lot on making sure each climber was being very precise with their foot placement. I noticed that sometimes this would result in people tensing up, climbing slower, and being generally more rigid in their movements. Ah, the placement is now perfect, but there is no weight on the foot! I call this the 'floating foot'.

Ultimately, good footwork has to serve the purpose of creating a platform for us to push off from and use our lower body. Perfect placement without load is pointless!

There are two main factors that influence how well connected the foot and foothold are:

- Whether you are exerting force on the foothold.
- Your body position.

APPLYING FORCE ON THE FOOTHOLD

This is as simple as it sounds – you have to actually apply force on the foothold. Most of the time, this means pushing down onto it or if you are on a steep overhang, clawing in. This is similar to creating a little bit of pressure to hold a piece of paper against the wall. The change may not be very visible; however, it should feel very different. When you push down on your foot, subtle but important changes happen to your centre of gravity and where you are creating tension within your body. If you're not doing this, do it. I call this step 'setting the foot'. It is crucial to do it before taking further action in the lower body (such as standing up or rocking over).

HOW BODY POSITION AFFECTS FOOT GRIP

The main relationship to note is:

- If your centre of gravity is above your foot, there will naturally be more weight over that foothold.

Practically, this means that unless we consciously do something with our body position, there will be more weight over the lower foothold than the higher foothold. This is, of course, a recurring problem, as we often want to step up onto the higher foothold to climb upwards.

When bringing a foot up, your centre of gravity is over the lower foothold and level with the higher foothold. As a result, there will naturally be more weight over the lower foothold than the higher foothold.

If we try to move up before there is enough weight on the higher foothold:

- the gung-ho who will 'just go for it' may experience a foot slip
- the strong are likely to pull themselves up with their arms, exerting great effort and strain
- the cautious who can sense that it is not a stable platform may not move at all.

The solution?

1. Set your foot by consciously pushing down on your higher foot. This usually creates enough initial grip to enable us to adjust our body position to further improve grip.
2. Do something to move your centre of gravity upwards.

We will go into greater detail of what you can do to move your centre of gravity upwards after pushing down with your foot in Chapter 10.

Before pushing down on the higher foothold

After pushing down on the higher foothold

FOOT SWAPS

Foot swapping is what we do when we need to swap, say, a right foot for a left foot on a foothold. Being able to do this well will vastly improve our options on the wall and make it less punishing if we do accidentally climb into the wrong position.

The goal of the foot swap is for both feet to be able to enjoy:

- the right part of each foot
- on the best part of the foothold
- with sufficient weight over the foothold.

There are three methods to foot swapping, but the basic principle is the same: simulate a controlled foot slip with the outgoing foot and mirror the action with the incoming foot.

Every foot swap is slightly different. Depending on the scenario, one of the methods above may be most suitable. Or you may need to use a combination of the three methods. Keep all three methods in mind and adjust according to each scenario.

METHOD 1: PIVOT OUT, PIVOT IN

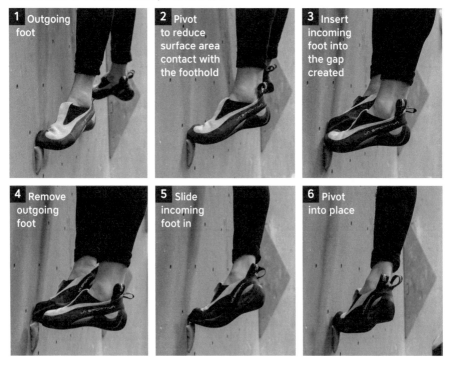

1 Outgoing foot

2 Pivot to reduce surface area contact with the foothold

3 Insert incoming foot into the gap created

4 Remove outgoing foot

5 Slide incoming foot in

6 Pivot into place

METHOD 2: DROP THE HEEL, POINT THE TOES

1 Outgoing foot

2 Drop the heel to disrupt the horizontal platform

3 Point the toes of the incoming foot to get into the gap created

4 Remove outgoing foot

5 Slide incoming foot into place

6 Establish stability on the foothold

METHOD 3: ROLL OUT, FOLD IN

1 Outgoing foot

2 Roll the foot outwards (supinate) to reduce surface area contact with the foothold – you can trace the outside rim of your shoe for support

3 Insert incoming foot at an angle

4 Remove outgoing foot

5 Fold foot into the gap (pronate) - you can trace the outside rim of your shoe for support

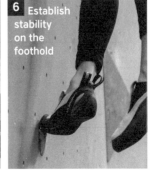
6 Establish stability on the foothold

EXPLORE

FOOT SWAPS

Give it a go on the wall.

1. Find a traverse wall.
2. Pick one of the three methods to start with.
3. Traverse in one direction, swapping feet as often as you can.
4. Traverse back in the opposite direction, swapping feet as often as you can.
5. Repeat the above using the other two methods.

PRACTICE MAKES PERFECT

Now it's time to bring all the different considerations of footwork together into one smooth climb.

THE GOLD STANDARD

Hold yourself to the gold standard, 100% of the time:

1. Place the right part of the foot...
2. on the best part of the foothold...
3. and have sufficient weight over it so we can push off from it.

Aim for all three of these steps for all the practice drills below.

It is important to push yourself to get your success rate as close to 100% as possible. This is because footwork is the foundation on which all other techniques are built. We need the feet to be stable and allow movement in order to access full function of the rest of the body. Of all the practice drills, these are the ones in which it is most important to push yourself to a high standard.

PRACTISE
WALKING

This drill will help you to make good footwork a habit.

1. Pick a reasonably dense part of the wall with at least two jugs for your hands.
2. Start in a base position using jugs.
3. 'Walk' from one foothold to the next, each time being mindful to achieve the gold standard.
4. Repeat until fatigued.

PRACTISE
FAST AND ACCURATE

This drill will help you to make good footwork a habit.

1. Pick a boulder problem, circuit, or route, ideally with small footholds, approximately one grade below flash level.
2. Go through all the individual moves, being conscientious about reading the foothold, taking more time to figure out the best option if needed.
3. Once you know the moves, repeat the climb – this time climbing it at your natural climbing pace.
4. Repeat another two or three times, each time trying to go a little faster while maintaining footwork quality.

SUMMARY

Wow, that was a lot of information about footwork!
Here's a table to recap:

Factor	Goal	Options
Reading the foothold	Identify the best foothold available and the best part of each foothold. Adjust foot placement to best fit the foothold profile.	Five key qualities: • Width • Depth • Direction • Slope • Texture
Foot placement	Be stable and allow hip movement.	Options: • Pivot point • Inner edge or outer edge • Smear radius
Connection between the foot and the foothold	Have weight over the foothold to create grip.	Options: • Push down on the foothold • Move the centre of gravity above the foothold
Foot swaps	Both outgoing foot and incoming foot can enjoy all three above points.	Options: • Pivot out, pivot in • Drop the heel, point the toes • Roll out, fold out • A blend of the above three Either way, the outgoing foot does a 'controlled foot slip.' The incoming foot mirrors the foot action of the outgoing foot.

Get the right part of your foot onto the best part of the foothold and make sure there is weight over it. Every single time. This is the foundation on which other techniques are dependent.

7

GRIPWORK

GET A GRIP

It's time to look at the more popular sibling of footwork: gripwork. What we are looking for is a secure grip to hang, pull or push off it.

Most of us use our hands all the time to do tasks that are far more fiddly than climbing and can intuitively make a good guess as to how to grab onto a hold well. So there isn't a great deal we need to consciously learn about gripwork (until we have mastered the fundamentals of climbing technique). The most important things to do here are to observe your handhold and work with its unique qualities.

READ YOUR HANDHOLD

These are the five qualities we are looking out for:

Width	How many fingers can you fit onto this hold?
Depth	How many knuckles deep is it?
Direction	Is it downward, side, or upwards loading?
Slope	Is it positive and in-cut or negative and sloping away?
Texture	Is it rough with good friction or smooth and shiny?

Width, depth, and texture are straightforward qualities – the wider, deeper, and rougher the hold is, the easier it is to secure your grip. Paying attention to these qualities helps you gauge the difficulty of the climb.

The more interesting qualities from a technique perspective are the direction and slope of each hold. These impact greatly what your base position is going to look like and the movement options that will be available to you.

DIRECTIONAL HOLDS
KEEP THE STRING TAUT

Let's start with what may seem like a random non-climbing exercise. We're going to try to draw a perfect circle using a piece of string and a pencil. First, attach a pencil to one end of a piece of string. Fix the other end to a point with a pin. Then, holding the string taut, draw a perfect circle.

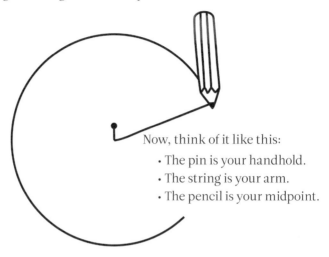

Now, think of it like this:
- The pin is your handhold.
- The string is your arm.
- The pencil is your midpoint.

You move your midpoint in such a way as to create a line of tension behind the handhold. We want to 'keep the string taut', just like in the exercise above. This is what keeps your weight on the handhold and creates a secure grip.

Moving whilst 'keeping the string taut

LEAN IN THE CORRECT DIRECTION

With downward-loading holds, the optimal line of tension is in the same direction as gravity, and that's why often we do not need to do very much to be secure. However, if the hold is angled in a more vertical direction (like a side pull) or is upside down (like an undercut), we need to consciously organise our midpoint to create a line of tension in the correct direction.

Leaning behind the most positive part of the handhold

DEVELOP
EQUALISING OVER THREE POINTS
(SIDE PULLS AND UNDERCUTS EDITION)

This exercise trains you to distribute weight over three points even in positions where it may not feel natural to do so.

1. Find a very hold-dense wall for this exercise.
2. Pick two good footholds that are roughly level with each other.
3. Keeping your feet on these two footholds, move from handhold to handhold using only handholds that are not downward loading. On each handhold, pause to form a stable triangle where you can take the other hand off and stay still.

IN-CUT VS. SLOPERS

Let's consider the slope factor. The main difference between an in-cut hold and a sloper is the number of directions you can load them in and still have a secure grip.

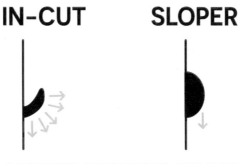

ACCEPTED DIRECTIONS OF LOAD

This influences which grip shapes we can use to hold them:

IN-CUT:

SLOPER:

In the move phase, we can continue to grip and control the movement for longer on in-cut holds than on sloper holds. In general, a sloper is a more difficult hold, as it accommodates fewer positions of stability and therefore demands that we position our body more precisely.

SLOPERS ARE SO DIFFICULT!

Here are four tips that can help you hold on to awful slopers:

1. Find the sweet spot
   Even the worst sloper has a weakness, and it's our task to find it! Search for the part of the sloper where it is least slopy and use that spot only. It may not be much, but trust me, it is going to make a difference.
2. Find your plumb line
   A plumb line is a weight attached to a string, and it's used to identify a straight vertical line. Imagine your hips are the weight and your arms are the string. When we find our plumb line, we are perfectly in line with gravity, and that is exactly where we want to be. Hold on to the sweet spot, find your plumb line, then put weight on the sloper.

3. Keep the hand and forearm stable

Ah yes, the great paradox: How do we move while keeping the plumb line? The simple answer is to keep the hand and forearm stable so this entire unit maintains the plumb line stable position. Bend at the elbow if needed, and the shoulder joint will allow upward movement. This tip is also relevant when using gastons, where you have to maintain grip tension in the opposite direction to the direction in which you are moving.

Keeping the hand and forearm stable

4. Be stealthy when you are moving

It is easy to throw yourself off balance with unnecessary adjustments. I know you are uncomfortable, but do not fidget. Fidgeting results in excessive movement and can create a lot of grip stress. Be stealthy and move decisively to the next handhold.

EXPLORE
SLOPER BASE POSITION

Give it a go on the wall.

1. Look for some slopers on a vertical wall (0-5° overhanging)
2. Use the above tips to try to get off the ground and find a stable base position using the sloper.
3. Move towards a nearby handhold.
4. Repeat on all the slopers you can find.

SUMMARY

Read the handhold by looking out for these features:

- Width
- Depth
- Direction
- Slope
- Texture

If the hold is on an angle:

- 'keep the string taut', meaning move your midpoint in such a way as to create a line of tension behind the handhold.

If the hold is a sloper:

- find the sweet spot on the handhold
- find your plumb line for balance
- keep your hand and forearm stable
- be stealthy when moving.

Otherwise, trust that your dexterous hands will figure out the most secure grip naturally!

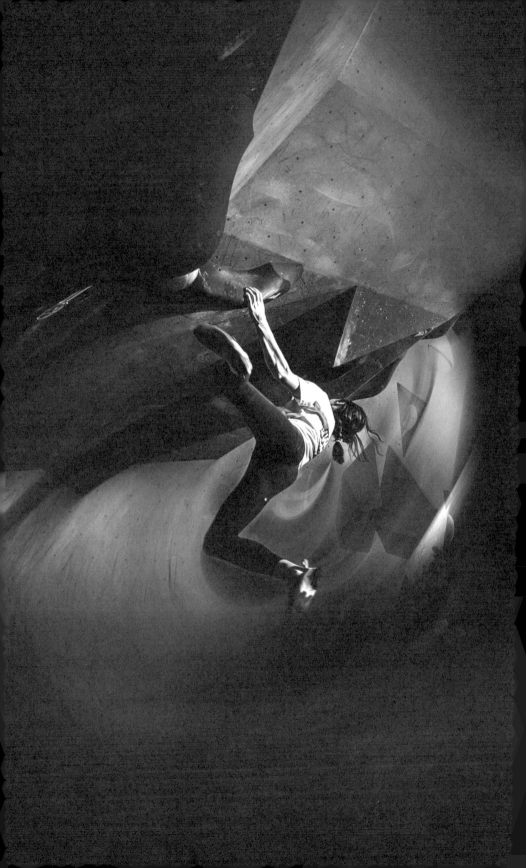

③

MOVE
PHASE

8

MOVEMENT FLOWS FROM THE BOTTOM UP

THE BOTTOM-UP PRINCIPLE

Each climbing move is a combination of multiple component movements. It is more complicated than a simple movement you might do in the gym, such as a squat or a pull up. When we have multiple component movements, we have to consider the sequence. Climbing well is about doing the right component movements in the right order. Getting the sequence right creates synergy and makes climbing feel easy.

Principle 3 governs the move phase:

• Movement flows from the bottom up.

This is what it looks like in practice:

1. Push down on your feet to ensure your weight is on them. If you are in a rest position, this step helps you establish the base position. If you are already in a base position, this step can sometimes still be helpful, especially when moving onto a poorer foothold. This helps to secure foot grip before making the weight transfer.
2. Use lower body action to move closer to the wall and gain height.
3. Use upper body action to carry forward upward movement. Ideally, we will start the upper body action just before the apex of the lower body action to create fluid movement. Reach with your arm at the apex of your upward movement.

Rest position

Set the feet to establish the base position

Lower body action

Upper body action

WHY DOES THIS MAKE CLIMBING EASIER?
SYNERGY

In this order of movements, each movement is making the next movement easier to execute. Stepping well creates a secure platform for your lower body to push off from. Pushing off from the lower body keeps the weight on the feet and strengthens the connection between foot and foothold. When you push off your lower body first, there is upwards momentum, and this makes the upper body action easier. This is similar to jumping into doing a pull up.

PROPORTIONALLY WORK THE STRONGER MUSCLES

Our lower body is much stronger and better developed than our upper body. Because we are bipedal animals, our lower body is equipped to handle our body weight in a way that our upper body is not. An effective use of the body is therefore to use our lower body to a greater proportion.

WELL-MEANING REBELS

Interestingly, many climbers who are conscientious about learning technique do not follow this principle. These are some common reasons why:

'CLIMBING IS ABOUT PULLING HARD'

There is a common perception that 'climbing is about pulling hard, which could lead to a misunderstanding of the importance of the lower body.

It is common to hear many high-level climbers say things like:

1. 'You have to pull harder.'
2. 'I'm focusing a lot on... (something about engaging the upper body).'

Many of us will look up to the best climbers for inspiration, and these statements can have a big impact on how we think about climbing. It is important to note that sometimes what the best climbers are saying to themselves may not be the most useful thing for you in your climbing journey right now. They are much further along the path and could be focusing on completely different skill areas.

Top climbers could be focusing on a lot of upper body action because:

• they have mastered the bottom-up sequencing and are working on developing the details of effective upper body action
• on difficult climbs, there is a limit to how much you can drive from the lower body, so there needs to be a significant contribution from the upper body.

We can see that: 'pulling hard' can be important, depending on the *context*. I think it is overly simplistic to say that 'you should not pull yourself up' or that 'climbing is mostly about your legs'. What's important is not whether you should be pulling with your arms but rather *when* and *how* to do it.

For most amateur climbers, it is probably less necessary to pull than they think. Most of us are very connected with our upper body (e.g., we do fiddly things with our hands like write, eat food, scroll on our phones) but less so with our lower body. When they start climbing, many people will be overly focused on what their upper body is doing and will not pay enough attention to their lower body.

STRESS RESPONSE

A common stress response is to tense up, especially in the shoulders and arms. When we are climbing, there are moments when we feel a spike in stress. For example, when we are above a big run out or when we are worried about others watching us climb. A classic stress response would be to hold your breath, tense your shoulders, and pull in with your arms. This can result in you unconsciously using your upper body to start the movements, even if you understand the bottom-up principle well.

The solution to this is awareness: check in regularly with your emotional state. If you notice yourself tensing up unnecessarily due to stress, take a moment to pause, reset, and breathe.

'BAD CLIMBING' TRIGGERED IN SPECIFIC POSITIONS

It is common for people to be able to do bottom-up climbing in some positions but not others. For example, many people can do it when they have two footholds but not when they only have one. It is also common for people to be proficient in only some of the wall angles. A typical example is being able to do bottom-up movement on vertical walls but not on steep overhangs.

If you have a specific style of climbing that you struggle with, start by checking whether you are following the bottom-up principle in this context.

COMMON MOVEMENT MISTAKES
POOR FOOTWORK

If your feet are not stable, your lower body does not have a secure platform to push off from. Good footwork is a necessary condition for executing the move phase well. See Chapter 6 for more information on footwork.

TOP-DOWN SEQUENCING

Using top-down sequencing instead of working from the bottom up is an incredibly common mistake. This means:

- first, pulling up in the upper body
- then pushing from the lower body
- and finally tensioning at the foot.

This creates a negative spiral of events where each action makes the next action harder. Pulling with the upper body tends to unweight the foothold. The de-weighting of the foot then makes pushing off from the lower body harder. Not pushing at the lower body then further de-weights the foot. This often results in either random foot slips or the need to exert excessive core tension to keep the feet on the footholds.

Top-down sequencing

Bottom-up sequencing

This strategy could work for you in the short term, especially if you are very upper-body strong. However, in the long run, it can cause multiple problems:

- It is inefficient.
- It rarely leads to success as climbs get more difficult.
- It increases the incidence of random foot slips. In addition to reducing success, this can result in a higher probability of injury due to the corresponding increased incidence of shock loading and uncontrolled falls.
- It increases the probability of upper body niggles and injuries (e.g., finger strains, elbow pain, shoulder issues) due to the higher workload on these structures.

NO PUSH FROM THE LOWER BODY

If you do not push off from your lower body, you do not move very much. This will inhibit your ability to do many climbs. If this sounds like you, I would revisit the comparison between the rest position and base position in Chapter 4, as this may be the root cause of the problem.

No push from the lower body

Pushing from the lower body helps to lift the entire torso

I'M TRYING BUT IT'S JUST NOT WORKING!

The funny thing about climbing is that it's easy to know the principles, but it's difficult to execute them! As the difficulty increases, we find ourselves in positions and on holds in which we feel it is impossible to push off from the legs. Part of the fun is figuring out how to apply the bottom-up principle.

In the next chapters, I will share more about how to keep applying the bottom-up principle in increasingly unreasonable positions.

SUMMARY

Each climbing move is a combination of multiple component movements. Climbing well is about doing the right component movements in the right order. Getting the sequence right creates synergy and makes climbing feel easy.

- Movement flows from the bottom up.
- What this means in practice:
  Set the feet → lower body action → upper body action.

9

LOWER BODY ACTION

THE STAR OF THE SHOW

The lower body is the star of the move phase. Everything that has been covered up to this point is important in so far as it sets the climber up to execute the lower body action well. Everything to follow is only possible when the lower body action is successful.

In this chapter, we will look at the fundamental techniques for moving the lower body:

1. Stand up
2. Rockover
3. Twist/drop knee
4. Squat

Before we go into the details of each technique, let's look at what we are trying to achieve with the lower body techniques.

REACH WITH YOUR BODY

Is this you?

Reaching with the arms

This is a classic case of what I call 'reaching with your arms'. This means that you are keeping your body still and straightening your arms in an attempt to get to the next handhold. This is a logical approach but a fairly limited strategy for climbing. This will only work for moves that are one arm's length away. To progress further in your climbing, you have to move the entire torso along towards the next hold before reaching out with your arms.

Reaching with the body

Imagine yourself as a cherry picker:

- Your legs and hips are like the main unit that elevates and controls movement.
- Your torso is like the work platform.
- Your arms are like the person on the work platform grabbing the cherries.

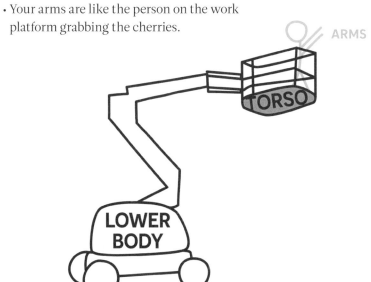

Raising your arms does not generate much reach. There is even less reach to be gained from bending the torso. You need to use your legs and hips to lift and transport your entire torso towards the next handhold. 'Reach with your body' is a cue to remind you to use your lower body to move, and not to simply wave your arms at the next handhold.

EXPLORE
ELBOW TOUCH

This exercise shortens your arm length, and so it will encourage you to reach with your body.

1. Use a climb you find reasonably easy.
2. On each move, try to touch the next handhold with the elbow of your reaching arm.
3. Afterwards, reflect on how that made you move differently.

DEVELOP
DOUBLES

This exercise encourages you to think of your lower body as the primary mover and practise aiming with your hips rather than your arms.

1. Use a climb you find reasonably easy.
2. Aim with your hips to move your body to the next position.
3. Let go of both handholds, and grab the next set of handholds with both hands.
4. Do this all the way to the top of the climb.

The rest of this chapter will explain the lower body techniques and how to execute them well. This is a good time to remind ourselves of Principle 5, 'Not too much, not too little, just the right amount.' Below I will describe the techniques and their component movements using images of the most classic forms of each technique. It will not look this way every time; that is to be expected and is normal. It's up to you, the climber, to adjust each component movement to suit each climb.

1. STAND UP
THE TECHNIQUE WITH NO NAME

Let's start with the most fundamental movement in climbing: standing up to move upwards. Yes, it really is as simple as it sounds! It's so mundane that the climbing world never even gave it a technical name. Funnily enough, that is also why it is so often overlooked. We start in a squat position, and we stand up to straighten the body. This gives us the reach to gain the handhold. We can then bring our feet up, return to a squat position, and repeat.

TRIPLE EXTENSION

Let's break it down further. Standing up in a climbing position is a little different from standing up from a chair. We tend to move simultaneously in three lower body joints, doing what is known as triple extension. This consists of:

1. tiptoe, or ankle plantar flexion
2. straightening the knees, or knee extension
3. hip thrust, or hip extension.

These three actions occur simultaneously. When done well, the movement feels smooth and powerful.

Here is an example of what it looks like:

| Base position (classic triangle) | Stand up | End position (square) |

In the base position, we are bent in these three joints. It is a perfect setup that allows us to triple extend and produce a lot of force to propel upward movement in the process. It can help to imagine your body as a bow and arrow: we pull back (squat down) to shoot up (stand up).

Let's have a look at the same image with a line overlay to see the movement more clearly. I want you to pay attention in particular to the angle changes in all three joints:

EXPLORE
TRIPLE EXTENSION ON THE GROUND
This exercise will help you to explore the triple extension movement in a simpler context.

1. Stand on the ground, with your feet hip width apart.
2. Squat down.
3. Stand up powerfully into an upright position on the tips of your toes.
4. Your goal is to finish in a stable position at the end of the movement (rather than falling over).
5. For variety, you can try these different versions of the same movement:
   a. Going fast
   b. Going slow
   c. Carry a weight

EXPLORE
STAND UP ON THE WALL
Give it a go on the wall.

1. Find a 0–15° wall.
2. Adopt a classic-triangle base position.
3. Stand up to gain the next handhold.

DEVELOP
ELIMINATES
This exercise will help you improve the quality of your stand up by encouraging you to get to full extension more often.

1. Pick a climb you find reasonably easy.
2. Aim to skip as many handholds as you can.
3. This will encourage you to stand up fully to get more reach.

2. ROCKOVER

We use the rockover technique to move sideways. When we rockover, our hips face the wall, and we move our centre of gravity towards the next handhold. In doing so, we bring our centre of gravity over the next foothold, transferring weight from one foothold to the next, making it more secure.

Here is an example of what a rockover looks like:

| Base position | Rockover | End position |

FIND YOUR HIP GLIDE

The key to a successful rockover is being able to glide your hips smoothly across from one side to the other. Let's start by getting to know the movement on the ground.

EXPLORE
ROCKOVER ON THE GROUND

This exercise will help you to explore the rockover movement in a simpler context.

1. Standing on the ground, take a wide stance with both feet pointing outwards.
2. Squat down, keeping the hips in external rotation so both knees are pointing outwards.
3. Glide from side to side.

Rockover on the ground

As you explore this movement, ask yourself:

1. Am I able to keep my knees pointing outwards throughout the movement?
2. Can I keep my torso upright?

These are the two necessary features of the rockover. We want to keep the knees pointing outwards, meaning the hips stay externally rotated, which enables us to transport our entire torso sideways. The torso needs to be reasonably upright. In climbing, the wall is in front of us and that's why we cannot pitch forward too much. If you are finding this difficult, then you might want to do some exercises to improve hip strength and mobility in external rotation. A quick YouTube search should bring up many fun options. Once you hit these two criteria, you can focus on improving execution:

• Does the movement feel smooth?
• How low can I go and still do this movement in control?
• How wide can I go and still do this movement in control?

The more we practise, the smoother it will be as the body learns to coordinate itself in this specific movement. The stronger and more mobile you are, the lower and wider you will be able to do this. Naturally, this will give you more options and control when climbing.

Now that you've found your hip glide, let's try it out on the wall.

EXPLORE
ROCKOVER ON THE WALL
Give it a go on the wall.

1. Find a 0–15° wall.
2. Adopt a classic-triangle base position.
3. Rockover to gain the next handhold.

SUPPORTING LEG PUSHES, LEADING LEG PULLS

It is useful to note that both legs are doing different actions in the rockover – one of them is the supporting leg, and the other the leading leg. The supporting leg pushes and extends to become straighter. The leading leg pulls in, deepening the bend at the knee to carry movement forward in the same direction.

This is the sequence of events:

1. The supporting leg pushes.
2. The leading leg pulls, and the hip glides over.

All three mechanisms should work synergistically to send your entire torso in the same direction.

Supporting leg pushes and extends

Leading leg pulls in and the hip glides over

Many climbers are not familiar with how to pull with their legs. To do this, we have to consciously claw in with the foot and pull in from the toe. We also actively use the muscles in the back of the leg, such as our calves, hamstrings, and glutes.

EXPLORE
FIND YOUR PULLING LEG
This exercise will help you to connect with the feeling of pulling in with your leg.

1. Standing on the ground, bring one foot in front of you.
2. On the front foot, push down on your pivot point and bring it towards your other foot. This step helps you to realise what the pulling action is in an open-chain format, which is a simpler context.
3. Now let's try it in a closed-chain context, which is what happens when we're climbing. Bring the same foot forward again. This time, pull in as you did in Step 2 while keeping your front foot on the same spot. This should pull your hips towards your front foot.

A smooth transition from push to pull transfers both weight and momentum seamlessly. A common mistake is to pause between the push and the pull. Pausing at the wrong moment in a move can feel awkward or you might even feel stuck. The goal for the rockover is to transition from push to pull continuously. The key word here is <u>continuously</u>. It is important not to obsess over doing the transition quickly. Aiming for speed often leads to rushing and poor execution of each component movement. Don't worry about speed. Focus on doing the transition continuously at a pace that feels right to you.

KNEES, KNEES, KNEES
My final piece of advice on rockovers is to bring awareness to your knees.

1. Are they locked out or are they bent?
2. What direction are they facing?

This may sound like obvious advice, but it should not be ignored. In my years of coaching, I have met many climbers who have very little awareness of their legs and knees while climbing. Yes, they are often caught by surprise themselves when I point this out! Many climbers will try to do a rockover with either a locked-out knee or the knees pointing inwards rather than outwards. This will restrict the entire movement. Setting up for the move correctly is a crucial step for success.

SOFT KNEES

Before you start a rockover, think 'soft knees'. Your knees can be slightly bent, or they can be straight, but they need to be ready to bend. It is very difficult to soften the knee joint once it is loaded. This means that once you shift your weight onto the leading leg, if it is straight and stiff, it is hard to correct it mid-movement. This is especially important for climbers who are hypermobile and can easily hyperextend or lock out in their knees.

A straight and stiff knee restricts the rockover

A soft knee enables a smooth rockover

BOTH KNEES POINT OUTWARDS

I mentioned this before, but it is very important: <u>both</u> knees should point outwards. Many climbers will think only of one leg and forget about the other.

If the leading knee is pointing inwards, it disrupts lateral movement towards the next handhold. The knee pointing inwards does two things:

- It naturally sends your centre of gravity in the opposite direction.
- It compels your entire hip to rotate to become side-on to the wall, disrupting the hip glide.

This is, in fact, the mechanism for the twist, which we will look at next. For the rockover, keep the knee pointing outwards.

The knee of the supporting leg should also point outwards so you are in a frog-like stance. This keeps both sides of the hip in external rotation and cohesively front-on to the wall. This is what makes the hip glide smooth.

Both knees pointing in the same direction

Both knees pointing outwards

DEVELOP
NO-HANDED WEIGHT SHIFT ON A SLAB

This exercise will help you practise rocking over without assistance from the upper body.

1. On a gentle slab, find two large footholds at a level stance.
2. Without using any handholds for support, rockover from side to side.

DEVELOP
GO STEEP, GO WIDE

Improve your skill in the rockover by exploring the movement in a more difficult context.

1. The steeper the wall, the more it will test your skill in the rockover. Improve the quality of your rockover by practising on a 30–40° overhanging wall.
2. The wider the stance, the more it will test your skill in the rockover. Improve the quality of your rockover by practising on progressively wider stances (footholds further away from each other).

3. TWIST/DROP KNEE
CLASSIC TWIST

Twisting is one of the most well-known techniques; it puts your body in a distinctive shape that is unique to climbing. We use this technique to move upwards in a very controlled way.

This is what a classic twist looks like:

Base position (classic triangle) Twist End position (square)

The most important action that we are trying to achieve with the twist is to turn our hips. In the base position, our hips are usually facing front-on the wall. We twist such that the hips become more perpendicular and side-on to the wall.

Base position   **End position**

To achieve this, we need to pivot on our toes, which should not be a problem if we are standing on our pivot point (see Chapter 6).

These are the other important actions that happen in a twist:

1. We shift our centre of gravity towards the handhold that stays on and so change our weight distribution from four points to three points. This creates stability.
2. We bring our midpoint closer to the wall and so gain height.
3. We rotate our 'free' shoulder upwards and so gain height.
4. We bring our chest closer to the arm that is holding on and so create stability in the upper body.

Many climbers will obsess about turning the knee inwards to get that super-classic 'twist look'. This is not as important as it seems. When the hip turns, the knee will naturally turn to one direction as well. If needed, after turning the hip you can rotate the knee in more to achieve a better position.

It is important to note that while there is height gain with the twist, it is much less than in the stand up. Therefore it is important to twist upwards, otherwise we will not be able to benefit from even the small amount of upward movement.

USE THE TWIST TO IMPROVE CONTROL

One of the biggest benefits of twisting is that we finish each twist in a stable end position while staying on the initial handholds and footholds. It is easier to pause at the top of the move compared with other techniques. Even when we are fully extended, our weight remains distributed over three points in a balanced way, and that allows us to be stable at the end position.

We finish each twist in a stable end position

This makes it an extra-useful technique for:
- doing static moves
- decelerating dynamic moves
- onsighting, when you do not know what your next handhold will feel like (or be!)
- going towards poor handholds.

OVERHANGS VS. VERTICAL FACES

The twist is most often employed on overhanging walls. There tends to be a lot of space between our hips and the wall when we are in the base position on an overhang. This means that:
- it is easy to turn our hips, as there is nothing in the way
- twisting can bring us a lot closer to the wall, and this improves how much potential reach we can gain.

In contrast, twisting on a vertical face or a steep slab can be less effective, as there is usually very little space between our hips and the wall when we are in the base position.

- If the wall is in the way, we may not be able to turn our hips without major adjustments to our body position.
- On angles very close to vertical, turning the hips may bring us further away from the wall. If so, it can result in reduced reach and disrupted balance.

EXPLORE
CLASSIC TWIST
Give it a go on the wall.
1. Find a 20–30° overhang.
2. Adopt a classic-triangle base position.
3. Twist to gain the next handhold.

DEVELOP
TWISTING ON AN OVERHANG
The steeper the wall, the more it will test your skill of twisting. Improve the quality of your twisting by practising on a 30–40° overhanging wall.

DROP KNEE
The drop knee is a particular variation of twisting where, in addition to turning the hip, we do a fair bit of internal rotation in the hip joint to 'drop the knee'. Because of the shape that our legs are now in, we have to push outwards on both feet to create the opposition force needed to grip with the feet. This is particularly useful for bunched positions where your footholds are very high relative to your handholds.

It's interesting to note that despite the multitude of movements in a drop knee, our centre of gravity does not move very much at all. That is why the drop knee is mainly used as a means to get stable and release an arm. The free arm can now either reach a nearby handhold or shake off and rest. The drop knee is also a very clever way of making use of footholds angled close to vertical or when climbing in a groove or corner feature.

| Base position | Drop knee | End position |

EXPLORE
90/90 ROTATIONS ON THE GROUND

This exercise will help you to explore internal and external hip rotation. It is also a good exercise for improving hip mobility and control.

1. Sitting on the ground, arrange your legs in a drop-knee shape. Both knees are pointing in the same direction and bent at around 90°. Keep your torso as upright as possible.
2. Pivoting on your heels, lift both knees up and rotate in your hips to point your knees in the opposite direction, then back to the ground.
3. Reverse the movement and repeat a few times.
4. Use your hands to support you on the ground if needed, working up to unassisted movement.

EXPLORE
DROP KNEE ON THE WALL

Give it a go on the wall.

1. Find a 20–30° overhang.
2. Adopt a classic-triangle base position.
3. Drop knee to gain the next handhold.

AFTER EVERY TWIST IS AN UNTWIST

It is important that we consider going both into and out of the twist. Because the twist locks us into a stable end position, it can be difficult to do anything else from here. We have to consciously untwist after we have achieved our target (the next handhold or rest) to re-establish the base position.

To untwist, we simply reverse all the movements we did in the first place:

1. Pivot at the toes.
2. Turn our hips from side-on to front-on and facing the wall.

And where necessary:

3. Externally rotate in one of our hips to return to a 'squat posture'.
4. Shift foot tension from pushing outwards to pushing downwards.

| End position | Redistribute weight to three points | New base position |

It is important to manage your weight in this process to remain in balance. Your weight should shift from behind the lower handhold to under the higher handhold. You can do this by changing the direction you are leaning in as you untwist.

| Leaning behind the lower handhold | Transition to leaning under higher handhold |

EXPLORE
UNTWIST ON THE WALL

Give it a go on the wall.

1. Find a 20–30° overhang.
2. Adopt a classic-triangle base position.
3. Twist to gain the next handhold.
4. Untwist to form a new base position with the higher handhold.

DEVELOP
CROSSOVERS

The more you reach over your other arm, the more your untwisting skills will be tested. Improve the quality of your untwist by practising crossover moves.

1. Find a 20–30° overhang.
2. Adopt a triangle base position.
3. Twist to gain a handhold on the other side of the staying hand.
4. Untwist to form a triangle base position.

4. SQUAT DOWN

Occasionally, we find that we need to move down. This is probably the least commonly used technique, but nevertheless, it is still extremely useful in very specific situations.

WHEN DO WE HAVE TO MOVE DOWN?

When we are downclimbing, of course! For boulderers, this is useful mostly as a way to reduce the risk and volume of big falls. For route climbers, this is very useful, particularly when onsighting, where we often climb up and down on hard-to-read sections to figure out what to do. It is also fairly common on traverse sections of climbs where we may move downwards for a move or two.

SQUAT DOWN

The main technique we use to move down is to squat down. If it looks like the reverse of the stand up, that's because it is. This is basically the same action as sitting down on a chair, so most of us are very familiar with it. There are very few problems with executing this technique because we are moving in the same direction as gravity is pulling us in. Most people find this quite intuitive!

| End position | Squat | Base position (classic triangle) |

The most common mistake I have noticed here is that many climbers try to control this movement with their arms rather than with their legs. When downclimbing, they create and keep a lot of tension in their upper body, as if they were doing the lowering down phase of a pull up. This is much more difficult and effortful and should be avoided. The upper body should be relaxed enough to allow the arms to straighten. The lower body should initiate and control the movement.

The other common mistake is the failure to align your centre of gravity with the lower handhold. Move your centre of gravity sideways so it's in line with your lower handhold before squatting downwards. This will reduce the chances of having to snatch at the next handhold or control a swing.

Keeping weight distributed in over four points (square)... can lead to a swing and shock loading on the way down

DEVELOP
DOWNCLIMBING
Give it a go on the wall.

1. Go up a boulder problem that you find reasonably easy.
2. Downclimb it.
3. Aim to control from the lower body so you can reach the next handhold in control.

CLASSIC COMBINATIONS
PICK AND MIX

All the techniques described above can be mixed and matched into as many combinations as you can imagine. It's not uncommon to start in a rockover, do a stand up, and finish in a twist. Here are some classic combinations to get you started.

CLASSIC COMBO 1: ROCKOVER INTO STAND UP

This is especially useful when we want to go diagonally upwards.

1. Start with the rockover to shift the weight onto the higher foothold.
2. Carry through the movement into the stand up to enable upwards movement.

Rockover into stand up

EXPLORE
ROCKOVER INTO STAND UP

Give it a go on the wall.

1. Find a 0–15° wall.
2. Adopt a classic-triangle position.
3. Rockover to one side.
4. Stand up as straight as you can.
5. Reach for the next handhold.

CLASSIC COMBO 2: STAND UP INTO TWIST

This is especially useful when we want to move upwards but decelerate at the end of the movement to grab the next handhold in control.

1. Start with a stand up.
2. Blend in the twist towards the end of the movement to continue corkscrewing upwards.

Stand up into twist

A less effective combination is to do these two techniques in the opposite sequence, starting with the twist and then standing up. Twisting puts the legs and hips in a more difficult position to stand up from and so can make it difficult to get to full extension.

Twist into stand up

EXPLORE
STAND UP INTO TWIST
Give it a go on the wall.

1. Find a 15–30° overhang.
2. Adopt a classic-triangle position.
3. Stand up to full extension.
4. Twist to stabilise your body.
5. Reach for the next handhold.

EXPLORE
STAND UP INTO TWIST VS. TWIST INTO STAND UP
This exercise helps you to understand how the sequence of techniques impacts your climbing efficacy.

1. Give both options a try
2. Which felt easier?

FRONT-ON AND SIDE-ON

You can categorise the above techniques into two families:

Category	Distinguishing factor	Techniques
Front-on (also known as: climbing open or square-on)	Hips face the wall throughout the movement	Rockover
Side-on (also known as: twisting)	Hips turn to become perpendicular to the wall	Classic twist/drop knee
Could be either front-on or side-on		Stand up Squat down

Thinking of the techniques in this framework can help you to process climbing movements more quickly and simplify decision making.

EXPLORE
FRONT-ON VS. SIDE-ON

This exercise helps you to understand the relative advantages and disadvantages of using front-on and side-on techniques.

PART 1: FRONT-ON ONLY
  1. Choose a climb that you find reasonably easy.
  2. Keep your hips facing the wall for the whole climb.

PART 2: SIDE-ON ONLY
  3. Use the same climb as above.
  4. Turn your hips on each move phase of the climb.

PART 3: COMPARE AND CONTRAST
  5. Which techniques were easier for which moves?

PART 4: THE PERFECT COMBO
  6. Repeat the same climb one more time, this time using the techniques that best fit each move.

THE SECRET SAUCE: EXTEND THE HIPS

Now that we know about the key techniques, we can talk about how to execute each of them well. The secret lies in developing a deep understanding of what your hips should be doing.

We should be extending the hips to move in towards the wall <u>at the same time</u> as standing up, rocking over, or twisting. The only exception is when downclimbing, where the hips move outwards. Hip extension is not a standalone technique but rather an essential component of the above listed techniques.

Let's take a closer look at our hip action when executing each of the three main techniques:

Stand up

Rockover

Twist

What do these images have in common? We extend the hips in all three scenarios. The angle of our hips increases – like when we flip open a laptop. We start with a smaller angle (knees closer to chest) and finish with a larger angle (knees further away from chest). If you've ever heard anyone shout 'thrust your hips in' or 'get closer to the wall', this is what they are referring to.

Why are the hips especially important?

1. The hip is one of the major joints in our body for expressing strength and is a great source of power and control. For example, hip extension is the main movement pattern in the deadlift. Most people can deadlift very heavy weights compared with other movement patterns such as the squat, leg press, or bench press.
2. When upright, your centre of gravity naturally sits just above your hip. An easy shorthand for comprehending movement is to think about the hips as the 'seat of your weight' and therefore more or less where your centre of gravity is. When we move our hips, we move our centre of gravity.

REACH ON THE IN

A useful cue to think about when climbing is: Reach on the in. In the move phase, when you are going towards the next handhold, your hips should be moving in towards the wall. When we move closer into the wall, we can access our full body length, and this enables us to gain height.

Getting close to the wall allows us to access our body's full length

Not moving into the wall during the move phase creates many problems:
- Often we do not gain enough vertical height.
- Even if we do gain sufficient height, we're often already falling away from the wall when our hand makes contact with the next handhold. This makes it difficult to hold the end position.

Reaching on the out

Reaching on the in

CUE THE HIPS

Here are some common climbing cues:

'Thrust your hips into the wall.'

'Get close to the wall.'

As we have discussed above, this is a very important movement. Unfortunately, I often hear this as well:

'You should always have your hips close to the wall.'

I hear this misunderstanding far too often when working with climbers. Your hips move both in and out of the wall, depending on which phase of the climb you are in. There can be no 'in' without an 'out'.

It is important to bring your hips into the wall:

- during the move phase
- when you are on a face climb or slab and your hips are sitting too far out from the balanced base position.

It is important to bring your hips away from the wall:

- to generate power before going for a move
- to re-establish the stable base position, especially on an overhang
- to bring your foot up to a high foothold.

The alternating stable–move rhythm can thus also be seen as the out–in rhythm.

Phase	Stable	Move	Stable	Move	Stable
Hip positioning	Out	In	Out	In	Out

This is, of course, relative positioning. For some climbs you will stay quite close to the wall in both phases, and for other climbs, the out–in movement will be across a greater distance. Let's not forget Principle 5, 'Not too much, not too little, just the right amount.'

THINK IN 3D

Let's take a moment to also remember Principle 4, 'Move in the correct 3D direction.' Many climbers, when they learn about the importance of hip extension, become completely obsessed and forget to think about it in three dimensions.

Thinking 'hips in' only

The correct 3D line for this move

SPECIFIC SCENARIOS THAT REQUIRE MORE HIP EXTENSION

These are some scenarios where we have to actively emphasise hip extension even more than usual:

1. Overhangs

   The steeper the overhang, the more we have to emphasise the hip extension. This is because the steeper the wall, the further away our hips tend to be in the base position. In order to move our hips through a greater distance, we need to exert more effort to extend the hips.

Hip action needed on a slight overhang   Hip action needed on a steep overhang

2. Moving from very bunched positions (e.g., using a high foothold or sit starts)

   When we are in a very bunched position, often our feet will be on footholds that are above our hips. The angle between our thigh and chest can be very small, making hip extension difficult. We have to channel more effort into hip extension to make any movements. When we emphasise hip extension, we also rearrange the relative hip position to bring the hips above the footholds, making upwards movement more feasible.

Sit starts: extend hips to get off the ground and establish base position

3. Using side pulls or undercuts

As we saw in Chapter 7, we want to adjust our body position so we can lean behind the most positive part of the hold. On side pulls and undercuts, we need our midpoint to be higher. Extending the hips lifts the entire hip unit higher, so we can lean behind our arms in the correct direction.

Staying low creates grip stress on side pulls

Extend the hips to lean behind the positive part of the handhold

EXPLORE
SEMI-SUPINE HIP BRIDGE

This exercise will help you to explore the hip extension in a simpler context.

1. Lie down on the floor facing the ceiling, with both feet on the ground and both knees bent at around 90°.
2. Keeping your shoulders and feet on the ground, lift your hips up so that they are fully extended.
3. Reverse the movement to return to the ground.
4. Repeat as needed to gain familiarity with this movement.
5. Harder variants might be useful, as we often do this movement in a much more complicated way on the wall. You can try doing the same movement with one leg only or with the hips in external rotation.

DEVELOP
SIT STARTS

1. There are usually two parts to a sit start:
2. Extend your hips to lift your bottom off the ground. This establishes the base position.
3. Now move off from the base position using the most relevant technique.
4. Doing lots of sit starts can help you to familiarise yourself with hip extension.

SUMMARY

Phew, that was a big chapter! I've summarised it all in a table below.

Which direction do you want to move in?	Technique	Component movements and sequence
Up	Stand up	Simultaneous triple extension: • tiptoe, or ankle plantar flexion • straightening the knees, or knee extension • hip thrust, or hip extension
Sideways	Rockover	Setup: • Soft knees • Both knees pointing outwards Sequence: • Supporting leg pushes • Leading leg pulls and hip glides
Move up in a very controlled way	Classic twist Drop knee	Setup: • Stepping on the pivot point Sequence: • Pivot on the toes • Turn the hip to become side-on to the wall • Turn the knee inwards if needed
In	Hip extension	A component of all above techniques. Particularly emphasised when on: • overhangs • bunched positions • side pulls or undercuts
Down	Squat down	Sequence: • Align centre of gravity with lower handhold • Squat down

To make this table useful as a problem-solving framework, I've categorised the techniques by their primary function in terms of single-direction movements. This makes it easier to remember and understand. But, of course, we are always moving in three dimensions.

Here is an example of how I would use the framework for problem solving:

- Say we are on a 20° overhanging wall, and I want to do a big reach to a handhold directly above my current handhold. In this situation, moving up is the most important requirement. And so, I decide to use the stand-up technique.
- On my first attempt, I manage to touch the bottom of the next handhold, but I feel that I am falling outwards as I touch it. Going back to my framework, I consider that I might have to emphasise hip extension more because of the overhanging nature of the wall.
- On my second attempt, I do the stand up again but this time more consciously thrusting my hips in. I touch the top of the next handhold before falling off.
- Again, returning to my framework, I think about adding a twist to help me to improve control.
- On my third attempt, I do the stand up, making sure to extend my hips like I did before, and then I twist just before my knees become straight. This time I can reach the hold and hold on. Hurray!

10
THE STAGGERED
STANCE PROBLEM

THE FAMILIAR TROUBLEMAKER

Now that we understand the main lower body techniques, we should discuss one of the most common obstacles to executing them well: the staggered stance. Luckily for us, this troublemaker behaves in a highly predictable manner. Let's get to know the ins and outs of this problem, and some tried-and-tested solutions.

The staggered stance

The staggered stance is the situation where both your footholds are not at the same height. The staggered stance may seem innocuous, but it is the source of many movement problems!

A level stance is when the two footholds in use are at roughly the same height. This is a simple place to be. Your centre of gravity naturally sits between your two feet, and weight tends to be fairly evenly distributed between these two footholds. This makes gripping and pushing down on these footholds straightforward. It's quite easy to move both legs as a cohesive unit, and you have the combined strength of both limbs to generate and control movement. Life is good!

This also means that you should make sure you keep an eye out for the level stance! Many climbers miss out on the benefits of the level stance by adopting a staggered stance when it is not necessary.

DEVELOP
LEVEL-STANCE HUNTING
This exercise is especially useful for climbers who find it difficult to decide which footholds to use.

1. Use a set climb for your handholds but allow yourself to use all the footholds available on the wall.
2. As you climb it, actively look out for a level stance every time you need to move your feet up.

In contrast, the staggered stance throws us off on so many fronts. When in our base position contemplating how to move, we are faced with three major problems:

1. Weight distribution
   Weight is unevenly distributed across both footholds. Typically, your centre of gravity will be above the lower foothold but either level with or below the higher foothold. This means there will be more weight on the lower foothold and less weight on the higher foothold. Left unmanaged, this could lead to:
   • a foot slip when you try to move onto the higher foothold
   • not enough height gained, as you did not get much out of the higher foothold.

Our centre of gravity sits in between the two footholds

2. Direction of travel

Your hips are above one foothold and below the other foothold. This creates a conflict in the direction of travel. Pushing off from the lower foothold sends you upwards, but pushing off from the higher foothold sends you outwards!

| The lower leg is set up to push upwards | The higher leg is set up to push outwards |

3. Ease of movement

The stance separates your legs and puts both legs in a shape that is close to the end of the joint range. The lower leg is almost straight and cannot contribute much movement. The burden of work is disproportionately on the higher leg, making it more about single-leg strength and control. Furthermore, the higher leg tends to be in a deeply bent position. Exerting from a deep bend is more difficult than doing so from a comfortable bend. Many of us don't have the strength to do a single-leg squat, let alone repeatedly on a climb!

| The lower leg is almost straight | The higher leg is deeply bent |

In general, the more staggered the stance (the greater the distance between both footholds), the more pronounced the problems will be.

Certain movement challenges may also be emphasised in specific climbs, for example:

- If the higher foothold is much poorer than the lower one, there will be a greater weight-distribution challenge.
- If we are going around an angle change such as a bulge or scoop feature, we may have a greater direction-of-travel challenge.
- If the stance is more staggered, we have a greater force-generation challenge.

Fret not – here are some tried-and-tested solutions to these challenges!

PSEUDO LEVEL STANCE

One simple solution is to imitate the level stance, even when you do not have the foothold available for it. You can simply smear with one foot on the bare wall where you would like to have a foothold.

| Staggered stance | Pseudo level stance | End position |

It's quite a clever trick really. By adopting the form of a level stance, we can mitigate two of the three problems created by the staggered stance.

1. Weight distribution
   When you bring the lower foot off the lower foothold and place it on the wall level with the higher foothold, you transfer some weight from the lower foothold to the higher foothold. Now you are more secure on the higher foothold and can use it more effectively.
2. Direction of travel
   We have to lift and level the hips to adopt a pseudo level stance. This usually repositions your hips above both footholds and resolves the conflict in direction of travel.

Sadly, it does not solve the last problem – ease of movement. The amount of support you get from a foothold is far greater than smearing on the bare wall. It remains difficult to generate force and control movement, as we still have to rely mostly on one leg to do this. The more supportive the smear is (and this varies with each climb), the easier it will be to move off from.

THE FOOT SQUISH

Smearing on the bare wall to create the pseudo level stance is not the same as the smearing we talked about in Chapter 6. This is because there isn't a protrusion for us to push down on, so we have to create this effect by pushing with our foot in a very particular way. I like to call this the 'foot squish'.

| First, push directly into the wall | Then push downwards | If you need to extend the ankle further, maintain some tension against the wall to keep the foot stable |

Pushing off in these different directions in sequence allows you to push down somewhat on the wall, and this makes the stand-up movement easier. This is not a very supported position, so it's important not to dawdle, as it can quite rapidly degenerate into a foot slip. Move decisively.

EXPLORE
WHERE SHOULD I FOOT SQUISH?
This exercise is about finding the best spot to foot squish. Where this will be is very individual and this is why this exercise is so useful.

1. Hold on to a jug with one hand, and step on to one good foothold.
2. Do the foot squish on different spots on the wall. Test each one out by trying to move off from each position.
3. Rank them in terms of ease of movement and foot security.

EXPLORE
PSEUDO LEVEL STANCE
1. Give it a go on the wall.
2. Find a climb that is reasonably easy for you.
3. Do the entire climb with the restriction of only using one foothold at a time.
4. Practise applying the pseudo level stance.

There are times when the pseudo level stance won't work, such as when the handholds are too poor and you have to keep the lower leg down to stay in balance. In these cases, the step up or the rockover are good alternatives.

STEP UP
The step up is a variant of the stand up. In the step up, we stagger the stand-up action in both legs to overcome the problems of the staggered stance. First, we stand up on the lower leg, then we stand up on the higher leg.

| Base position | Lower leg stands up | Upper leg stands up |

Let's zoom in and look at the steps needed for each phase.

PHASE 1

Lower leg initiates

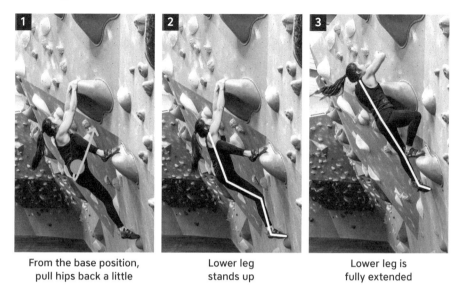

| From the base position, pull hips back a little | Lower leg stands up | Lower leg is fully extended |

PHASE 2

Higher leg carries through the movement

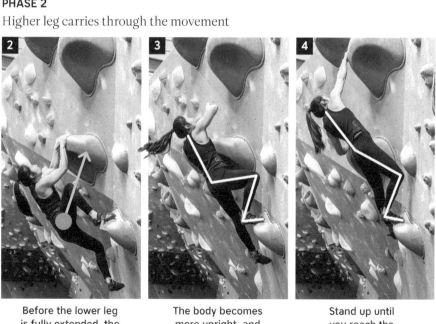

| Before the lower leg is fully extended, the higher foot begins to pull in to assist in the weight transfer | The body becomes more upright, and it becomes easier to stand up on the higher leg | Stand up until you reach the end position |

A well-executed step up solves all three problems of the staggered stance:

1. Weight distribution
   In a staggered stance, there is naturally more weight over the lower foothold. This is why we start the lower body action here. When we stand up on the lower leg, we lift our centre of gravity and the weight shifts onto the higher foothold. Now there is weight over the higher foothold, and this provides the necessary grip for us to push off and extend the higher leg.

2. Direction of travel
   In a staggered stance, extending the lower leg will push us upwards, and extending the upper leg will push us outwards. When we start at the lower leg, we lift the entire torso, changing the hip-to-foot relationship in the upper leg. Now the hip is above the higher foothold, and so extending the upper leg will also push us upwards.

| Phase 1 | Phase 2 | End position |

3. Ease of movement
   In a staggered stance, the lower leg tends to be in a more upright position – usually with the hip above the knee and knee above the foot. In contrast, the higher leg is in an almost inverted position, where your hip is below the knee and the knee is only just higher than or level with the foot. When we initiate from the lower leg, this lifts the entire torso, recreating the relatively upright position on the higher leg and simultaneously putting it in a less stretched-out position. This makes it feel easier to extend the higher leg.

With multiple mechanisms at play, the step up can make a move go from feeling impossible to feeling easy!

The secret to a successful step up is to harness synergy by timing the movements well. We want to connect the initial movement seamlessly to the next movement. The smoother the transfer of energy – the smoother the movement will be and the less effortful it will feel.

EXPLORE
STEP UPS ON A BOX
This exercise will help you to explore the step up in a simpler context.

1. Find a plyometric box or any sort of stable stool.
2. Place one foot on the top.
3. Practise doing the step-up movement.

EXPLORE
STEP UPS ON A WALL
Give it a go on the wall.

1. Find a slab or up to 10° wall.
2. Adopt a staggered stance triangle position.
3. Step up and reach for the next handhold.

DEVELOP
STEP UPS ON A SLAB
This exercise will help you to improve the quality of your step ups by removing all support from the upper body.

1. On a slab, find a good foothold that is around your knee height.
2. Step up onto this foothold and finish in a balanced no-handed position.

DEVELOP
ELIMINATES (LOOK FOR STEP UPS)
We did this exercise in Chapter 9, but this time we are going to focus on stepping up from staggered stances. There is more potential for height gain in a step up from a staggered stance than a stand up from a level base, as you can use higher footholds.

1. Find a climb you find reasonably easy.
2. Aim to stand up fully on the higher leg. In the process, skip as many handholds as you can.

ROCKOVER

The method for rocking over in the staggered stance is very similar to that used in the level stance; it simply requires a greater level of skill and conviction to make it successful.

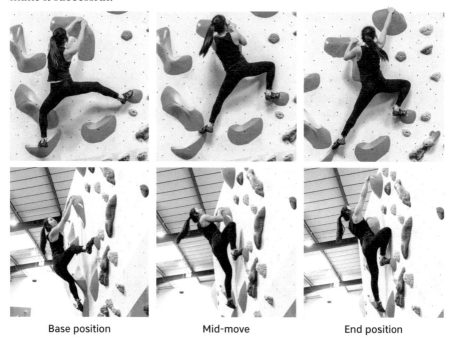

Base position   Mid-move   End position

Each component of the rockover will have to be executed to a higher level.

1. You may need to push off from the supporting leg with more force than in a level stance. There is a higher threshold to cross – you need to both level the hips and make sure you get your hips above your higher foot.

2. In the leading leg, you have to pull more, especially if the lower leg is almost completely straight. This involves more intentionally clawing in with the foot, extending the hips, and pulling with the back of the leg.

Clawing in with the foot throughout the entire rockover movement

3. For the hip glide, we need to consciously level the hips to achieve a smooth glide.

The hips are tipped at the initial position   Level the hips as you glide over

BE CLEAR ABOUT YOUR END POSITION

Now that the stakes are higher, we have to be clearer about the target end position. Do we want to finish in a sit in or a stand up?

Rockover into a sit in   Rockover into a stand up

We decide which to use based on where the next handhold is.

Rockover to...	Sit in	Stand up
Where is my next handhold?	Horizontally to the side	Diagonally upwards
At the end of the rockover, I am in...	A very stable rest position	A slightly bent active-squat position I can stand up from; it's usually best to transition to the stand up in a continuous way

It is important to be clear about which one you need before you start, as it is difficult to change course midway through the movement. Once you are in a full sit in, it can become extremely hard to stand up. Similarly, it can be difficult to pause midway through a stand-up move, so you might overshoot and miss the next handhold.

EXPLORE
ROCKOVER TO SIT IN VS. STAND UP
This exercise helps you to get familiar with the differences between a rockover to a sit in and a rockover to a stand up.

1. Find a 0–15° wall.
2. Try a rockover into a sit in and then a rockover into a stand up.
3. How were they different? How were they similar?

SUMMARY

The staggered stance is a problem because it causes issues with:

1. weight distribution
2. direction of travel
3. ease of movement.

Here are some tried-and-tested solutions:

Solution	What is it?
Pseudo level stance	Setup: Bring the lower leg up to the wall to create a level stance. Use the foot squish to smear on the wall. From here, stand up, rockover, twist, or squat as you would in a level stance.
Step up	Sequence: 1. Stand up on the lower leg. 2. Stand up on the higher leg.
Rockover	This is basically the same as the level stance version, but a higher level of skill is required. Sequence: 1. The supporting leg pushes. 2. The leading leg pulls and hip glides. Be clear on what your target end position is: is it a rockover into a sit in or a rockover into a stand up?

11

UPPER BODY ACTION

PASS THE BATON

It's time to pass the baton on to the upper body. In each move phase, the lower body initiates and the upper body completes the movement.

In this chapter, we will look at the various upper body pulling and pushing techniques:

1. Pull and pivot
2. Pull down to the front
3. Pull down to the side
4. Pull into a bent arm (including lock off)
5. Straight-arm push and pivot
6. Bent-arm push

I will also explain how to match the right lower body technique with the right upper body technique.

PULLING
TO PULL OR NOT TO PULL

Two pieces of advice about pulling are commonly heard in the climbing community:

> We often hear instructors working with beginners saying, 'You shouldn't pull with the arms at all,' and, 'Hang on your skeleton.'
> And on the other side, while grunting and power screaming up the hard boulders, 'Squeeze hard, pull hard, try hard!!!'

It's time to resolve this contradiction. Below, I will respond to both viewpoints and explain why I think neither of these camps is providing useful advice.

'YOU SHOULDN'T PULL WITH YOUR ARMS AT ALL'

I have seen many climbers who follow this advice wholeheartedly, and incredibly, they manage to climb holding virtually no tension in their shoulders at all. It may sound like they've turned themselves into the ultimate efficient climbing machine, but unfortunately it results in them hanging really low on their shoulders. It is mechanically quite difficult to do various shoulder movements from this end-range overhead position. As a result, instead of standing up in control, they swing to generate movement, even for small moves. It is quite difficult to generate the precise amount of swing, especially for a climber who is trying not to exert at all. Often the climber overshoots and 'crash-lands' on the next hold, repeatedly shock loading their arms in a completely unsupported shoulder position! Many people find harder moves impossible from this low hanging position.

Initiating movement with a swing

Crash landing on the next handhold

Initiating movement with a stand up

Grabbing the next hold in control

'SQUEEZE HARD, PULL HARD'

It might be easy to see why this is not a long-term strategy. Yes, it is important to regulate how much exertion and force you are producing. To do a bigger move, or to move from a less supported position, often requires you to exert more. Unfortunately, what often underlies this 'try hard' approach is a 'more is more' mentality, which often misses the nuances of how, how much, and when to pull. The 'pull harder' approach may help you climb harder things in the short term, but applying brute force in a blunt way rarely leads to long-term or meaningful progress. There are certain movements that require a more delicate touch, where the cue might even be 'don't pull'. It's important to recognise when this is the case. Regardless, continually 'pulling harder' comes at a great physical cost. Many advocates of this idea often battle with overuse-related arm injuries or pain in their shoulders, elbows, and/or fingers.

THE MORE USEFUL QUESTION...

It is usually more useful to ask yourself:

When should I pull?
The answer is always: After you push off with your lower body.

The next useful question is:

How should I pull?
The answer is always: It depends.
What does it depend on? Well, that's what the rest of this chapter is about.

PULL FROM THE SHOULDER

There are many ways to pull ourselves up with our upper body. What is common across all the ways to pull ourselves up is to control the pull from the shoulders and back.

Controlling the pull from the shoulders and back

This is why pulling from the shoulders and back is beneficial:

- It uses the bigger and stronger muscles in our shoulder and torso such as the latissimus dorsi, trapezius, and serratus anterior.
- The shoulder is a ball-and-socket joint and therefore capable of pulling in many different directions. The potential is immense!
- It enables us to pull with a straight arm, giving us access to our full arm span.
- It makes the pull into a bent arm stronger. When we start the pull in the shoulders and then carry it through to the arms to bend the elbow, it becomes a much stronger movement. The first movement stabilises the shoulder girdle and so synchronises the torso muscles with the arm muscles, enabling you to pull more easily.

Controlling the pull from the arms and neck

Conversely, controlling the pull from the arms and neck is less effective:

- The muscles in our arms such as the biceps and triceps are smaller and weaker.
- Pulling from our arms without stabilising at the shoulder girdle can be mechanically inefficient and often leads to straining at the neck. This can increase the incidence of shoulder and neck pain.
- We have to bend the elbow, which means we can only pull in very few directions. Bending our elbow also shortens our reach.

| Pulling from the shoulders and back | Pulling from the arms and neck |

Many people will pull from the arms because they do not have good awareness of their shoulders and have difficulty controlling movements from this joint.

EXPLORE
SHOULDER BLADE MOVEMENTS

This exercise is to help you explore how your shoulder blades move. In either standing or sitting, try doing each of these movements:

1. Arms forward, reach forward, and then backwards.
2. Arms down along your sides, shrug up, and then draw down.
3. Arms down along your sides, hunch forward, and then open your chest.

We saw in Chapter 4 the importance of adopting an active base position instead of a passive rest position. One of the main reasons for positioning yourself in an active hang in the base position is that it puts the shoulder in a supported position where it is relatively easy to pull from. Remember that in climbing we are doing most of the heavy lifting with our lower body (see Chapter 8). Relatively little upward movement is generated from upper body pulling, especially for lower difficulty levels. This means that, although we are talking a lot about pulling in this chapter, you may not have to do very much of it at all!

CREATE SYNERGY WITH THE LOWER BODY

Because movement flows from the bottom up, the upper body must complement the lower body action to create synergy. The two key elements impacting execution are:

- direction
- timing.

Direction is simple. Both the lower body and upper body action should move your torso in the same direction. For example, if we want to move upwards, we stand up and pull down.

Base position

Not able to reach the next hold as the upper body and lower body are pulling the torso in conflicting directions

Base position

Comfortably reaching the next hold when the upper body and lower body move in unison

Timing is more of an art. Typically, we want to start the movement from the lower body and start pulling just before we reach the apex of the lower body action. This carries through the initial momentum to link both movements seamlessly. Experience and practice are essential to honing this skill to a high level.

Base position	Pulling in with the upper body too soon	Not able to reach the next hold
Base position	Pulling in with the upper body at the right time	Comfortably reaching the next hold

Now let's have a look at the pulling techniques and how they are usually used:

1. Pull and pivot
2. Pull down to the front
3. Pull down to the side
4. Pull into a bent arm

1. PULL AND PIVOT

Pull and pivot

We usually pull in and pivot around at the shoulder blade to complement a twist. When we twist, we need to pivot at the shoulder to enable rotation. There is relatively little to do, as the lower body drives the movement. All we are trying to achieve with the upper body is to get the shoulder to sit in a place where it is comfortable and easy to pivot. After you twist your chest towards your arm, you can pull in at the shoulder a little to secure the position and give you more stability.

EXPLORE
PULL AND PIVOT

This exercise will help you to explore the pull-and-pivot movement in isolation.

1. Start in either standing or sitting.
2. Bring one arm forward in front of you, palm facing inwards. This is the pulling arm in this exercise.
3. Place the other hand on your chest with your index finger in your armpit.
4. Pull your shoulder blade back and down until the inside of your pulling arm is touching the hand on your chest.
5. Repeat until familiar, then switch sides.

EXPLORE
LOADED PULL AND PIVOT

This exercise will help you to explore the pull-and-pivot movement in a simpler context and under load.

1. Using a single suspension strap, gymnastic ring, or a bar at chest height, adopt a inclined pull up position. In this position, your body should be horizontal underneath the equipment, both feet at hip width on the ground. You are facing up to the ceiling, and holding on with one arm.
2. Open up at the chest so that your arm and your chest are open at 180°.
3. Pull in with your shoulders to bring your chest up to 90° and then continue pivoting until your chest is touching your arm.
4. Lower to the starting position in control.
5. Repeat until the movement feels familiar, then switch sides.

2. PULL DOWN TO THE FRONT

Pull down to the front

We often pull down to the front when moving up. It usually follows the stand up or the step up. The straight-arm version is especially useful on:

- overhangs, where you have a lot of space between yourself and the wall
- size 2 moves, where we need to straighten our legs to full, or close to full, extension; this allows us to maximise access to the full length of both our arm span and height
- very small moves, where not much movement needs to happen at all and we are already in a straight-armed base position.

3. PULL DOWN TO THE SIDE

Pulling down to the side

We pull down and to the side when we are moving diagonally upwards. It usually follows the rockover. Keeping the arms straight allows us to move sideways and reach further.

A slight bend to the elbow can be useful to maintain tension along the arm. However, bending deeply at the elbow can often inhibit movement in these scenarios, as it is literally pulling you in the opposite direction!

EXPLORE
STRAIGHT-ARM PULLS
This exercise will help you to explore the straight-arm pull movements in a simpler context so that you can better understand it.

LOW RESISTANCE:
1. Using either a resistance band attached to a bar, or a cable machine, explore each straight-arm pull:
   a. Down to the front
   b. Down to the side

HIGH RESISTANCE:
1. Using a bar, explore these straight-arm pulls with two arms:
   a. Down to the front: front tuck lever
   b. Down to the side: first half of the wide pull up

OPTION TO PULL INTO A BENT ARM
We can choose to pull into a bent arm in all the above pulls. It is most useful in the following scenarios:

  • When we need to keep the elbow low to maintain grip on our handhold.

Pulling into a bent arm to maintain grip on the left hand

For example, on this move, the left hand is a downward-loading flat hold. To maintain grip throughout the move, I have to keep the elbow below the handhold, so I bend my elbow in order to continue my upwards movement. Nevertheless, I am controlling the pull primarily from my shoulders.

- When we want to finish in a position where the torso is close to one arm. This is also known as the locked-off position.

| Base position | Locked-off end position |

The lock off is strongest when the chest is very close to the locking arm. This shortens the lever significantly, making it a stable position to be in. When we are carrying a heavy weight, it is easier to hold it close to the torso than with an outstretched arm. The same principle is at work here. Pulling in with the arm to bend the elbow helps us to adopt this stable position.

EXPLORE
PULL UP ON A SLOPER OR OPEN-HAND GRIP
On a sloper or open-hand grip, we have to keep the elbow low in order to maintain grip. Doing pull ups from these grips will teach us to pull from the shoulder while still bending at the elbow. To make this easier, keep your feet on the ground but do not push with your legs.

DEVELOP
ROCKOVER LOCK OFFS
This exercise will help you refine both the rockover movement and the locked-off end position.

1. Find a wall of 0–15° on a reasonably easy climb without any big moves.
2. Rockover and finish in a stable locked-off position, pausing to touch the next hold before holding on to it.

If you executed the rockover well, the legs will be actively working, and you will have brought your body into a stable end position. This will make it a lot easier to hold a lock off and make it possible for you to pause. The pausing thus becomes a form of feedback on your movement quality.

REVERSE THE ABOVE TO DOWNCLIMB

When we are downclimbing, we have to do the opposite of pulling. Instead of creating tension, we release tension to allow the arm to move upwards (That is, relative to your body. In practice, it stays on a fixed point, which is the handhold.) If you are coming from a bent arm, release tension first in the arms and then the shoulders. The lower body controls the descending movement. Direct your arm so it complements the direction of travel.

PUSHING

Another important upper body movement is pushing. We don't do it as often as pulling, so it can be overlooked at times.

We use pushing most often on lower-angled walls such as slabs, heavily featured face climbs, corner features, and mantling over the top of a bulge. In these situations, pushing with an arm can fulfil the same function as pushing with a leg.

The other common usage on all angles is as part of the V-shaped triangle (see Chapter 12).

PASSIVE VS. ACTIVE SHOULDER POSITION

A good push starts with a good setup position. This is an extension of the principles we talked about in Chapter 4. Where possible, we want to start each push in an active supported position where it is easy to push from.

For many years, I had shoulder pain whenever I did any pressing movements. I finally had a breakthrough when I did my Pilates teacher training course: I realised I was always pushing from an unsupported shoulder position! The classic characteristics of a passive unsupported position are as follows:

- The top of your shoulder has risen and is very close to your ear.
- You are not able to turn your head freely.
- Your arm is pressed up against the side of your torso.
- The top of your shoulder is rolling forward.

The active position we want to start in looks like this:

- The top of your shoulder is comfortably staying level with the collar bone.
- You can turn your head freely.
- There is a gap at your armpit, so your arm is not in contact with the side of your torso.
- It feels quite open at the chest.
- There is a line of tension running from your armpit to your arm.

Passive push position

Active push position

Passive push position

Active push position

EXPLORE
SIDE PLANK LIFTS
This exercise will help you to explore the active push position in a simpler context:

1. Start by lying on your side, propped up on one arm.
2. Start in the passive push position and push down on your palm to establish the active push position.
3. Lift your hips to go into a conventional side plank hold.
4. Reverse the movement in control.
5. Repeat until you are familiar with the various shoulder positions.

We want to control the movement predominantly with our shoulders. Starting from an active supported position makes it easier for us to execute this principle. The benefits mirror the ones we mentioned in the pulling section:

1. It uses the bigger and stronger muscles in our shoulder and trunk such as the latissimus dorsi, pectoralis, and serratus anterior.
2. The shoulder is a ball-and-socket joint and therefore capable of pushing in many different directions. The potential is immense!
3. It enables us to push with a straight arm, giving us access to our full arm span.
4. It makes the push from a bent arm stronger. Pushing from the shoulders first stabilises the shoulder girdle, and so synchronises the torso muscles with the arm muscles, enabling you to push more easily.

With this principle in mind, let's get into the specifics of the pushing techniques:

1. Straight-arm post and pivot
2. Bent-arm push

1. STRAIGHT-ARM POST AND PIVOT

This straight-arm post is about creating a line of tension down the entire arm so it acts as a single unit (as if your elbow didn't exist). We focus on changing the angle at the armpit to create movement. A cue that can be helpful here is to think of it as 'stacking the joints' to form a 'flag post'. The shoulder can now function as a pivot point, and we move our body around it.

Straight-arm post and pivot

EXPLORE
PILATES TWIST

This exercise will help you to explore the straight-arm post and pivot in a simpler context.

1. Start by lying on your side, propped up on one arm.
2. Push down and lift your hips up into a side plank position.
3. Reach up overhead with your free arm and then twist down to touch your opposite foot.
4. Reverse the movement to return your hips back to the ground.
5. Repeat until the movement feels fluid and familiar.
6. Repeat on the other side.

PRACTISE
STRAIGHT-ARM POST AND PIVOT

Give it a go on the wall.

1. Find a corner that has some large flat holds that you can press off from.
2. Put your left foot on a foothold and right hand on the other side of the corner (or vice versa).
3. Push up with the lower body.
4. Post and pivot to gain a higher handhold.

2. BENT-ARM PUSH

Sometimes we find that we need to push from a bent-arm position. The principle is the same as pushing from a straight arm:

1. Push from the shoulders to adopt an active push position.
2. Carry through this movement into the arms, straightening the elbow.
3. A straight-arm post is quite a secure position to finish in, so the goal of the bent-arm push is often to finish in a straight-arm post.
4. From here, if needed you can carry on to do the post and pivot discussed above.

As always, the lower body should be doing the heavy lifting here, sending your centre of gravity upwards. The pushing arm plays only a supporting role.

Place left arm in a bent-arm
push position

Push down to establish
an active push position

Stand up and push into a
straight-arm post

Straight-arm
post and pivot

EXPLORE
PUSH UP INTO PILATES TWIST

This exercise will help you to explore the bent-arm push in a simpler context.

1. Start in a prone position, with your hands next to your shoulders.
2. Do a regular push up.
3. Transition into the Pilates twist described above.

EXPLORE
BENT-ARM PUSH

Give it a go on the wall.

1. Find a slab or a corner.
2. Start in a stable bent-arm position.
3. Rockover with your lower body.
4. Push into a straight-arm post position.

COMMON USES
CORNERS AND SLABS

We often do push actions when we are in corners or on slabs. These wall angles create many opportunities for pushing, even when there are very few protrusions. We can keep our torso relatively upright when pushing, and this complements the slab base position very well.

Pushing is commonly used in corners and slabs

TOPPING OUT

Pushing down on a hold is also known as 'mantling' in climbing. Mantling over a bulge is a very challenging task. This is also known as topping out. It is difficult because we have to transition from a pull into a push in the upper body. Here, it is important to execute Principle 3, 'Movement flows from the bottom up'. Effective standing up or rocking over is what allows us to offload the pull and flip the hand to turn it into a push.

A typical top out sequence:

Rockover and pull
downwards with
the arms

The right arm continues to pull
downwards. The left arm shifts
into a bent-arm push position

The left arm pushes from a bent-
arm into a straight-arm post. This
shifts the weight off the right arm

Rearrange the right
arm into a bent-
arm push position

Stand up and push with the
arm into a straight-arm post

Continue to stand up and
pivot around the right arm

Bring the right foot up

Establish your new base position

PUSH TO FORM A V TRIANGLE

Another useful application of the push is to create a wider base of support along the shoulder line to establish a V-shaped triangle. This stabilises the body when we want to bring a foot up to a higher foothold. We will go into this in more detail in the next chapter.

Pushing to form a V triangle

SUMMARY

The two main things we do with our upper body are pulling and pushing.

Pulling
- Pulling is part of climbing. Ask yourself: When? How?
- Pull from the shoulders and back for more strength, control, and movement options.
- Create synergy with the lower body action with precise direction and refined timing.
- Pulling options and the usual pairings:

Lower body action	Upper body pull
Stand up Step up	Pull down to the front
Rockover	Pull down to the side
Twist	Pull and pivot
Squat	Release tension and allow the arm to move upwards

- Pull with a straight arm to maximise reach.
- Pull into a bent arm to:
  a. maintain grip on a handhold
  b. finish in a locked-off position.

Pushing
- Pushing is common on slabs, heavily featured face climbs, corners, and going around bulges.
- Push from an active supported shoulder position.
- Push from the shoulders first, even when coming from a bent-arm position.
- Techniques:
  a. Straight-arm post and pivot
  b. Push from a bent arm into a straight-arm post
- Common uses:
  a. On low-angled walls such as slabs, corners, and vertical faces
  b. Topping out/mantling over a bulge
  c. To form a V triangle and bring a foot up

4
CLOSING THE LOOP

12

RETURN TO BASE

FROM AN END TO A NEW BEGINNING

In Part 2, we explored the initial stable phase, and in Part 3 the move phase. The topics we have discussed so far take us from the base position to the end position.

| Base position | Mid-move | End position |

To carry on climbing from the end position, we have to bring our feet up to higher footholds to form a new base position. From here we can then do the next move. Bringing feet up is the final step that closes the loop and creates a repeating pattern.

In this chapter, we will look at the various techniques and adjustments for bringing a foot up:

1. V triangle
2. Going swiftly
3. Adjustments to help you bring a foot high

V-SHAPED TRIANGLE

At the end of a move, we are often in a 'square' shape, with weight distributed over four points. To release a leg to move it onto the next foothold in a stable and controlled way, we need to redistribute weight to three points. (Yes, this is the same principle we talked about in Chapter 4!) The difference here is that we want to distribute weight across the two handholds and one foothold to form a V-shaped triangle. The V triangle frees up a leg so we can reposition our foot on a higher foothold and establish a new classic triangle at a higher stance.

V triangle

REDISTRIBUTE WEIGHT

In order to redistribute weight from four points (square) to three points (V triangle), we have to move our centre of gravity. This is usually a small movement and can be easily overlooked.

Square   V triangle

Missing out this step can be problematic for two reasons:

1. It can result in an excessive amount of swing that is difficult to control.

Square   Removing the right foot   More effort is required
                          results in a swing   to control the swing and
                                                         gain the next foothold

2. When we are not in balance, we often create more tension in the body to establish stability. This creates rigidity and can inhibit movement.

Square   Unable to get to the
                          next foothold

Redistributing weight to form a V triangle is a simple and effective way of solving these problems.

V triangle

Remove the right foot without disrupting stability

Place right foot on to the next foothold with ease

V triangle

Place your foot on the next foothold

GO WIDE TO IMPROVE STABILITY

The V triangle is not a particularly stable position. We can usually hold this position momentarily with some effort, but it can very quickly feel effortful and unstable. This is because:

1. your base of support is above your centre of gravity, so you have to use body tension to keep yourself in place
2. you're predominantly on the upper body, which is, of course, weaker than the lower body.

The V triangle enables control and stability but not rest. Its main function is to create enough stability so that we can bring a foot up to establish a higher base of support. You can improve stability by creating a wide base in the arms. Generally, the wider the base, the more stable your V triangle will be.

What will swing less when you push it – a pendulum or a necklace?

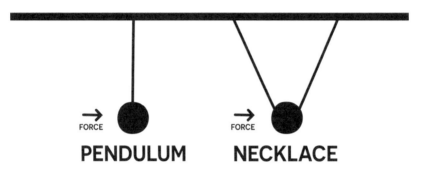

PENDULUM   NECKLACE

If there is only one handhold available, you can still go wide by pushing against the bare wall with your other hand. This sounds precarious, but it can be surprisingly stable and effective!

Pushing against the wall to form a V triangle

EXPLORE

V-TRIANGLE DRINKING GAME

This exercise is about developing your observation skills and pattern recognition.

1. Look up an uncut video of your favourite climber.
2. Drink (score a point) every time they form a V triangle.

DEVELOP

WALKING ON THE WALL

This exercise trains you to distribute weight over three points even in positions where it may not feel natural to do so.

1. Find a very hold-dense wall for this exercise.
2. Pick two good handholds:

    a. We want to focus on your understanding of positional complexity, so stick to jugs to avoid adding too many other factors into the mix.

    b. The easiest version would be with two handholds that are roughly level with each other.

    c. The harder version would be with two handholds in a staggered setup.
3. Keeping your hands on these two handholds, move from foothold to foothold, each time pausing to form a stable V triangle where you can take the other leg off and stay still.
4. Challenge yourself to use footholds at increasingly outrageous locations and see if you can make it work.

PRACTISE

FIND YOUR V TRIANGLE

1. This exercise trains you to regularly form V triangles.
2. Pick a climb that is relatively easy for you.
3. As you climb up, pause each time you need to move your foot up and find a V triangle. If you find a good position, you should be able to take off one leg without destabilising the rest of your body.
4. Repeat the same climb, this time climbing it at your natural pace, making sure to visit the same V-triangle positions you found previously.

IF NO STABLE POSITION IS AVAILABLE, GO SWIFTLY

Sometimes it won't be possible to create a stable enough V triangle where you can pause and remove a foot without swinging off. In these situations, we make do with what we have. Do your best to distribute more weight towards a V triangle shape, then swiftly move your foot to the new foothold.

The key to moving swiftly and precisely is preparation. While you still have four points of contact, look at your next foothold so you know exactly what you are aiming for. Ready yourself, and in one swift motion, relocate your foot to the next foothold.

Eyeing up the next foothold

Go swiftly

BRINGING A FOOT HIGH

How often have you struggled to bring a foot up to a higher foothold? When faced with this problem, many climbers hastily conclude that it is a hip-mobility issue and proceed to sign up for yoga classes. Hip-mobility is, of course, important, but first, let's make sure we're not missing out on some crucial positional adjustments!

If you try to touch your toes from standing, is it easier to do so with...

1. bent knees or straight knees
2. a curved spine or a straight spine
3. your knees pointing forward or pointing outwards?

The answer is the first option for all three questions. It is easier to touch your toes from standing with bent knees, a curved spine, and knees pointing forward! We want to apply this knowledge on the wall. The more joints we can bend to lift the leg, the easier it will be.

There are four adjustments you can employ to make it easier to bring a foot up:

1. THE RIGHT BODY SPACING

If we are very stretched out, there is little opportunity to curve the spine. When stretched out, we also tend to be very close to the wall, which means there is less room to bring the leg up in front of us. This forces us to lift the leg up in full external rotation, which requires a high degree of hip mobility. In this case, it may be better to walk both feet up in small steps before bringing your foot up to the target foothold.

Being too stretched out and unable to get to the target foothold

Using an intermediate step makes it possible to get to the target foothold

The same can happen if you are too bunched up, especially on slabs or vertical walls. To stay in balance in a bunched position, the hip has to be in external rotation. This forces you to lift the other leg in full external rotation, which is much harder. In this scenario, it may be better to walk the feet down to your previous foothold before bringing up a high foot.

Bringing a foot up from a bunched position requires a lot of hip flexibility

Walking the feet back down makes it easier to get to the target foothold

2. LEAN AWAY FROM THE WALL

After you've achieved the right body spacing, the next step is to lean away from the wall. Specifically, you are trying to create space between your belly button and the wall. This will allow you to curve the spine and bring the leg up more directly in front of you.

Staying close to the wall and unable to reach the target foothold

Leaning away from the wall makes it possible to get to the target foothold

3. STANDING UP WITH THE LEG

We can also straighten the leg that remains on a foothold. When we do so, we lift the entire hip unit higher, reducing the distance by which we need to lift the other leg up. In this scenario, try to stand up without getting too close to the wall. If you end up too close to the wall, it will reduce your opportunity to curve in the spine and bring the knee up in front, thus negating the height gain from standing up.

Staying low and unable to reach the target foothold

Standing up makes it possible to get to the target foothold

4. TURN TO BE SIDE-ON

The final trick is to pivot to be side-on to the wall. This circumvents the need to go into external rotation and reduces the demand for hip flexibility.

Staying front-on and unable to get to the target foothold

Turning to become side-on makes it possible to get to the target foothold

EXPLORE
HOW HIGH CAN I GO?
This exercise will help you to understand how the different positional factors affect how high you can bring your foot up.

VERSION 1: DISTANCE FROM WALL
1. Stand on the ground next to a wall. Your toes should be right up to the wall and facing forward. Hold on to a handhold for support.
2. Keeping your belly button as close to the wall as you can, bring one foot up and note where you can get to.
3. Now lean away from the wall, keeping your hand on the handhold, and your feet in the same location. Bring one foot up and note where you can get to.
4. Which is higher? How much difference did it make?

VERSION 2: TOES FORWARD VS. TOES POINTING OUTWARDS
1. Stand on the ground next to a wall. Your toes should be right up to the wall. Hold on to a handhold for support.
2. Keep your toes pointing forward, and bring one foot up as high as you can. Note where you can get to.
3. Now, rearrange your feet so that they form a V shape. Both heels and the side of your big toe should be as close to the wall as you can manage. Bring one foot up as high as you can and note where you are able to get to.
4. Which is higher? How much difference did it make?

DEVELOP
FOOT TO HAND
This exercise will help you to improve your ability to bring your feet high.
1. Find a climb that is reasonably easy for you.
2. Climb it with the restriction that you have to bring a foot to your lower hand before you can move your hand off it.

SUMMARY

At the end of each move phase, we need to bring our feet up to a higher footholds to form a new base position. This step closes the loop and now we have a repeating pattern!

To bring a foot up:

- Where possible, form a V triangle. A wide base in the arms makes this more stable.
- If a stable V triangle is not available, be prepared to go swiftly.
- To make it easier to bring a foot high:
  1. Find the right body spacing.
  2. Lean away from the wall.
  3. Stand up with the other leg.
  4. Turn to be side-on.

5

PUTTING IT ALL TOGETHER

13
A SERIES OF REPEATING PATTERNS

RECOGNISING PATTERNS

This is the fun bit – putting everything together to see the big picture. I hope that you can now see how climbing is made up of a series of repeating patterns.

**Base position
(classic triangle)**

**Mid-move
(Lower body: stand up
Upper body: pull down)**

**End position
(square)**

**Bring foot up
(V triangle)**

**Bring foot up
(V triangle)**

**Base position
(classic triangle)**

The basic rhythm of climbing is an alternating pattern of stable and move:

STABLE	MOVE	STABLE	MOVE	STABLE	MOVE

This is an abbreviated version of what we want to do in each phase:

Phase	STABLE	MOVE		STABLE			
What is my body doing?	Base position	Lower body action	Upper body action	End position	Bring foot up	Rest position (optional)	Base position

We can expand it further to see how the relevant techniques fit in:

Phase	STABLE	MOVE		STABLE			
What is my body doing?	Base position	Lower body action	Upper body action	End position	Bring foot up	Rest position (optional)	Base position
Options	Classic triangle	Stand up/ step up	Pull and pivot*	Square	V triangle	Classic triangle	Classic triangle
		Rockover	Pull down to the front*	V triangle	Go swiftly		
		Twist	Pull down to the side*				
		Squat	Straight-arm post and pivot				
		A combination of the above	Bent-arm push				
			A combination of the above				

*Option to pull from a straight arm or into a bent arm.

On a slab, it is pretty much the same, with some specific adjustments:

Base position
(two-point platform)

Mid-move
(step up)

End position
(one-point platform)

Base position
(two-point platform)

Bring a foot up
(one-point platform)

Base position
(two-point platform)

Phase	STABLE	MOVE		STABLE		
What is my body doing?	Base position	Lower body action	Upper body action	End position	Bring foot up	Base position
Options	Two-point platform	As above	As above but more likely to do pushing than pulling	Classic triangle	V triangle	Two-point platform
	One-point platform			Two-point platform	One-point platform	One-point platform
				One-point platform		

And now let's zoom out again to see the big picture. This is a visual representation of an entire climb, where we repeat this pattern over and over again until we get to the top!

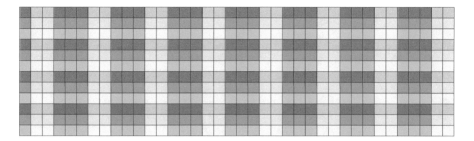

SUMMARY

Climbing is a series of repeating patterns. Get to know the component parts, and repeat.

14

PROBLEM SOLVING

SAY 'NO' TO TRIAL AND ERROR

Climbing is a dynamic activity that requires us to actively observe, assess, and problem-solve; it isn't like following a recipe or a set of instructions for flatpack furniture. Every climb is different, and we need to adjust our knowledge to the specific requirements of each climb.

A common mistake climbers make is to start their first attempt with their personal favourite technique instead of choosing the technique that best meets the requirements of a climb. If their favourite technique doesn't work, they then work down the list to their next favourite technique or just anything else they can think of. This is an inefficient method of problem solving based on trial and error. I believe the reason that so many climbers do this is because there are so many techniques in climbing that it is hard to get your head around them all!

A SYSTEMATIC PROCESS

Don't get lost in the chaos. Here's a simple four-step process you can use for problem solving:

GIVE IT A GO

OBSERVE WHAT YOU DID

ANALYSE YOUR SITUATION

COME UP WITH AN IDEA

Why do I like this framework?

- It is systematic, so you are less likely to repeat the same mistakes.
- It gives space for both rational analysis and an intuitive, feeling-it-out approach. Both modes of problem solving are important, especially in a movement-based activity.
- It is simple, so you can probably remember what to do.
- It is progressive, meaning that you can build on the knowledge gained from previous attempts.
- There's no specific 'starting point' – you can jump in anywhere!

Let's walk through how this works in practice and see how it ties in with everything we've discussed in previous chapters:

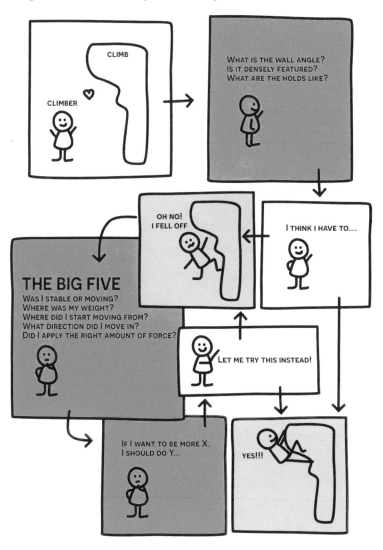

We cannot know what we have yet to experience. And so, it follows that we cannot expect to route read perfectly on climbs we have not yet tried. Even when you can do a climb on your first attempt, you can usually find an easier method after putting in several more attempts. The more difficult a climb is relative to our climbing ability, the harder it will be to correctly identify the techniques and specific adjustments needed before we attempt it. This is why problem solving is a very important skill to develop.

Following a systematic problem-solving process is simple but can be tedious. Here's a reason why it is absolutely worth the effort: effective problem solving is the gateway to progress. It enables us to discover and learn new movements. It hones our judgement by correcting misconceptions and refining crude estimates. This is how we convert experience into skill.

SUMMARY

Follow the simple four-step process to problem solve and avoid the dreaded trial-and-error method:

1. Give it a go.
2. Observe what you did.
3. Analyse your situation.
4. Come up with an idea.

And repeat.

Stick with it: problem solving is the gateway to progress.

15

SELF-ASSESSMENT AND PRACTICE GUIDELINES

WHAT SHOULD I DO NOW?

We've covered a lot of topics in this book, and it can be difficult to know where to start. Furthermore, developing each skill to a high standard takes time, focus, and energy. This is why it is important to have clear priorities.

This chapter will guide you to:

- Identify your growth areas through self-assessment.
- Prioritise your growth areas so you know where to start.
- Organise your priorities to build a progressive technique programme.
- Incorporate technique practice into every climbing session.

SELF-ASSESS

Below is a checklist to help you self-assess your climbing.

There are a couple of ways you can approach this:

1. Go through the table and fill it out based on gut feeling. The simple act of going through it and reflecting on your climbing should help you improve self-awareness and give you some ideas on which areas to focus.
2. Fill out the table below once based on gut feeling. Then film yourself climbing and fill it out again based on what you see on the videos. Aim for at least ten different boulder problems, or five routes, at a moderate difficulty level. This would be something you can complete in one to five attempts. It will be interesting to see if there is a difference between the first version of your completed table and what the videos show you.

Topic	Do I...?	Often or when it is needed	Yes, but rarely or reluctantly	No, I avoid it	I don't know
The Big Five	Have clearly defined stable and move phases				
	Pay attention to where my centre of gravity is				
	Know what I am holding on to and stepping on to (points of contact)				
	Know which of my points of contact are weighted				
	Know where I initiate movement from				
	Consider all three dimensions of direction				
	Know my line of travel				
	Aim to land lightly on the next hold				
Route reading	Pay attention to the wall angle				
	Pay attention to how densely featured a climb is				
	Accurately estimate what I can reach with bent and outstretched limbs				
	Pay attention to the profile of my handholds and footholds				
	Remember what I was doing when I fell off				

Body positioning (0–40°)	Differentiate between the rest position and the base position				
	Distribute weight over three points to form a classic triangle				
Body positioning (slab)	Stand upright on a slab				
	Distribute weight over my feet to form a stable platform				
	Move my arms and head freely				
Footwork	Step on the pivot point when I need to pivot				
	Step on the edges when I need extra support				
	Feel stable on smears				
	Pay attention to the features of a foothold				
	Have weight over my foot				
	Understand what causes a foot slip				
	Know how to foot swap without hopping				
Gripwork	Pay attention to the features of a handhold				

	Adjust my midpoint according to the direction of the handhold				
	'Keep the string taut' while moving				
	Feel stable on side pulls				
	Feel stable on undercuts				
	Feel stable on slopers				
Kinetic sequence	Start my movement from the bottom up				
Lower body action	Stand up				
	Rockover				
	Twist				
	Drop knee				
	Emphasise hip extension at the right moments				
	Squat down				
	Combine the above in weird and wonderful ways				
Staggered stance	Hunt for level stances				

	Know how to form a pseudo level stance				
	Step up				
	Rockover on a high foothold				
	Combine the above in weird and wonderful ways				
Upper body	Have awareness of my shoulder blade movements				
	Control my pull from the shoulders				
	Pull and pivot				
	Pull down the front with a straight arm				
	Pull down the side with a straight arm				
	Pull down the front into a bent arm				
	Pull down the side into a bent arm				
	Start pushing from an active supported shoulder position				
	Post and pivot around a straight arm				
	Push from a bent arm				
	Combine the above in weird and wonderful ways				

Closing the loop	Form a V triangle to bring my feet up				
	Search for a wide stance in the arms				
	Know how to go swiftly to bypass the V triangle phase				
	Search for the right body spacing before bringing my foot up				
	Lean away from the wall to bring my foot up				
	Stand up with the leg to bring my foot up				
	Turn side-on to bring my foot up				
	Re-establish my base position after each move phase				
Big picture	Understand how climbing is a series of repeating patterns				
Problem solving	Problem solve in a systematic way				

PRIORITISE YOUR GROWTH AREAS

To progress, it is best to target your gaps in understanding. These are the items in the table that you marked with 'I don't know' or 'No, I avoid it'. These are the areas that are likely to lead to the most growth if you work on them (your 'growth areas'). I recommend starting at the top of the table and working your way down. I have organised it in this way so you can plan your programme easily.

SKILL DEVELOPMENT PATHWAY

There are four phases to progress through for each technique.

PHASE 1: EXPLORE

The best place to start is to bring awareness to where you are at and have a few exploratory goes. Use the 'Explore' exercises for this.

PHASE 2: DEVELOP

The next step is to develop your movement skill. Progress your practice in this order:

1. Learn to execute the technique to a high standard in the easiest context available to you. Move on to the next step when you can reproduce this standard reliably.
2. Introduce variation by practising the skill in different situations (for example, on a different wall angle, or using a different grip type). Pay attention to subtle adjustments that make the movement feel smooth and effective. It is usually more productive to tackle one variation at a time (i.e., if you are changing the wall angle, do not change the grip type as well). Move on to the next phase when you can execute the technique across all the variations within the same difficulty grade.

PHASE 3: PRACTISE

Use repetition to build familiarity so that you can execute the technique intuitively. For some techniques, I have included 'Practise' exercises. Otherwise, the best way to practise is to repeat climbs that challenged you in this particular technique.

PHASE 4: JUDGE

The final step is to hone your judgement. Pay attention to the underlying principles of each technique to deepen understanding. This will help you to correctly identify when to use this technique.

Before each climb, take time to read the route. Did your estimate match up with the eventual solution? Make a mental note each time, regardless of success or failure, to build up your database and hone judgement.

ORGANISE YOUR PRIORITIES

The first two phases of the skill development pathway are the most demanding in terms of mental focus, physical effort and time needed. Focus on one technique at a time during these phases.

	Technique 1	Technique 2	Technique 3
Phase 1	Current focus		
Phase 2			
Phase 3			
Phase 4			

When you reach phase 3, you can introduce the next priority and work on two techniques simultaneously.

	Technique 1	Technique 2	Technique 3
Phase 1	Completed	Current focus	
Phase 2	Completed		
Phase 3	Current focus		
Phase 4			

Phase 4 is the least demanding, but takes the longest time to master. It's fine to have multiple priorities running simultaneously here. Doing so has a positive effect as you will learn to discern between the different techniques and how they are best used.

	Technique 1	Technique 2	Technique 3	Technique 4
Phase 1	Completed	Completed	Completed	Completed
Phase 2	Completed	Completed	Completed	Current focus
Phase 3	Completed	Completed	Current focus	
Phase 4	Current focus	Current focus		

WHEN TO PRACTISE

My go-to approach is to do focused practice on your growth areas at the start of every climbing session as part of your warm-up. Here are some good reasons why:

- If you practise specific movements at the start of the session, you are more likely to use these movements later in the session.
- It is an easy habit to build, and this improves consistency.
- It adds interest to what might otherwise be a boring section of your climbing session.

I have included exercises you can use for your practice in each chapter. Aim for 5–20 minutes of practice in each session. You don't have to spend a long time on it to produce results, but it does have to be good-quality, focused practice.

After a period of focused practice, put whatever you are working on to the back of your mind and go enjoy climbing anything you want! Return to the ideas in this book as and when you get stuck on a project and are searching for inspiration.

We learn so much through play, socialising, and carefree experimentation. This is an invaluable part of climbing – both for enjoyment and progress. Focus is important, but we can only really focus on one thing at a time. The combination of a focused start and playful curiosity for the rest of your session allows us to enjoy the best of both worlds.

SUMMARY

Have clear priorities so you can give enough attention to developing your skill in each technique.

- Self-assess to identify your growth areas.
- Prioritise your growth areas according to the table so you know where to start.
- There are four phases to skill development. Progress your technique programme in this order:
  1. Explore
  2. Develop
  3. Practise
  4. Judge
- Practise at the start of every session.
- Stay playful, stay curious :P

A FINAL WORD...
LEARNING NEVER ENDS!

There are many topics that we have not discussed. Here's a non-comprehensive list:
- Force quality (e.g., explosive power, slow controlled movements, creating rigidity)
- Timing (e.g., deadpointing)
- One-foot-on techniques (e.g., flagging)
- Cut-loose moves and dynos
- Heel hooks, toe hooks, and knee bars
- Compression
- Pacing

In Chapter 3, we explored a framework that categorises and organises all climbing movement. Let's see which topics in this table have not been covered by this book.:

Movement topic	Breakdown	Techniques
Rhythm	1. Stable 2. Move	Having distinct phases Classic stable–move rhythm Non-classical rhythms
Body position	1. One-point platform 2. Two-point platform 3. Classic triangle 4. V triangle 5. Opposite side 6. Same side 7. Two-point hang 8. One-point hang	Rest position Base position End position
Kinetic sequence	Set the feet → lower body action → upper body action	Movement flows from the bottom up
Direction of travel	Three dimensions: up/down, left/right, in/out	Stand up/step up Rockover Twist Hip extension Downclimb
Wall angle	1. Slab 2. Slight overhang 3. Steep overhang 4. Roof	Adjust body position accordingly

Size of move	1. Size 1: The next handhold is within reach with all three contact points remaining in their initial places. 2. Size 2: To reach the next handhold, one foot must leave a foothold. This category includes reaches up to one body length. 3. Size 3: To reach the next handhold, both feet must leave the footholds. The lower hand remains on the initial handhold. 4. Size 4: To reach the next handhold, all four points must leave the initial handholds and footholds.	Static moves: 1. Small reach move Dynamic moves: 2. Full extension move 3. Cut loose move 4. Dyno
Gripwork and footwork	Size, profile, and direction of holds	Pivot point Edging Foot swaps Side pull Undercut Sloper Gaston Crimp Pinch etc.

The topics I chose for this book are those I consider to be the most fundamental aspects of climbing technique. These fundamental aspects will serve as a good foundation for further development. Needless to say, there are plenty of questions left unanswered. Keep an eye out for Volume 2! You can stay up-to-date with my work at: xiangoh.com.

APPENDIX

Here are a few additional climbing sequences to illustrate the movement system.

Base position
(classic triangle)

Move phase
(Lower body: twist
Upper body: pull
and pivot)

Body spacing
adjustment (bring
right foot down)

Bring foot up
(V triangle)

Bring foot up
(V triangle)

Base position
(classic triangle)

**Base position
(classic triangle)**

**Move phase (Lower body:
rockover and step up
Upper body: pull down to the
side and bent-arm push)**

**End position
(square)**

**Bring a foot up
(V triangle)**

**Bring a foot up
(stand up and lean away)**

**Base position
(classic triangle)**

Base position
(classic triangle)

Body position adjustment
(foot swap)

Base position
(classic triangle)

Move phase (Lower body:
stand up and twist
Upper body: pull and pivot)

Base position
(classic triangle)

Move phase (Lower body:
rockover and stand up
Upper body: pull
down to the side)

Base position
(two-point platform)

Move phase
(rockover)

End position
(classic triangle)

Base position
(classic triangle)

Move phase
(stand up)

Bring a foot up
(V triangle)

Base position
(staggered stance)

Base position
(pseudo level stance)

Move phase
(Lower body: stand up Upper
body: pull down the front
'keeping the string taut')

End position (square)

Bring a foot up (V triangle)

Base position
(classic triangle)

ACKNOWLEDGEMENTS

THE FOUNDATION

Thank you to everyone I've ever coached. Thank you for your trust and sharing your climbing with me. It is through coaching and getting to know so many of you that I developed my understanding of climbing technique.

THE PRODUCTION TEAM

Producing this book has been a team effort. I am so grateful for my amazing team, whose expertise and professionalism I admire greatly:

- Photography: Charlotte Bull
- Cover design: Chris Luk
- Video filming: Annie Martin
- Copy edit: Bonnie Craig
- Book interior design: Simon Thompson

Every climber needs a wall! All images were taken at these fantastic walls, check them out:

- The Climbing Hangar Reading
- Hang. Climbing Centre
- HarroWall Climbing Centre

This book started as an idea back in 2019. I started writing and quickly realised I did not know enough to produce a book. I spent the next four years obsessively trying to fill in the gaps. A big thank you to Ross Gray who was my main 'sparring partner' during this period, throwing ideas around and sharing with me his immense knowledge of movement.

MY SUPPORT CREW

I am so lucky to be surrounded by supportive family and friends:

My husband Nick for taking on all the roles I needed from you – climber, business partner, proofreader, husband. Thank you for having the maturity and grace to keep me steady through the ups and downs even when I was asking too much from you. Thank you for your unwavering belief in me right from the beginning. You inspire me everyday.

Aaron Tan for opening my eyes to what good technique is way back when we first started climbing. Thank you for advising on the first draft, especially on the technical areas. There is no one I respect more to comment on technique. It is through you that I realised how beautiful climbing could be. Thank you for your friendship, I cherish it deeply.

My family for your excitement and your strength. The last 18 months have been difficult, and we are finding our feet again. Thank you for giving me the space to pursue this dream.

THE FINAL PUSH

I started writing again in August 2023. This time the words poured out, and it still felt like a mammoth project! A huge, huge thank you to the people who helped me, cheered me on and kept me going to the finish line.

Everyone who read the first draft and sent comments to help me make it even better:

- David Gudmundsson
- Eve Blumson
- Asha Patel
- Chee Wong
- Simona Dagyte
- Gerard O'Reilly
- Lukie Tolhurst
- Barney Light
- Ben Wilkins
- Ellen Zhang
- Kostas Georgakopoulos
- Gabby Myers
- Danielle Harper
- Justin Harper
- Olivia Pocock
- Joe Nathan
- Natasha Brown
- Luke Colgan
- Barnaby Russell
- Dipika Hopkins
- Anna Diaz-Price
- Annie Martin
- Tom Wright
- Joe Partridge
- Sam Prior
- Sam Green
- Lindsey McKerrell
- Hannah Lee

Special thanks to Holly Edgar for the pep talk exactly when I really needed it!

ABOUT THE AUTHOR

Xian is a climber, coach... and now writer! She lives in Berkshire with her husband and two home boards. She started climbing in 2005 and still loves it as much as day one (maybe more!).

Xian likes the idea of having multiple identities. She has competed internationally representing Singapore, does all the outdoor disciples, and wouldn't say no to a run, jump and kick. She enjoys trying hard, but also recently learnt that she likes climbing even more than she likes being good at climbing.

Xian ~~loves sunshine and long walks on the beach~~ loves having more projects on the go than is humanly possible to achieve. There's nothing quite like the intense stress of not knowing what to do and the sweet satisfaction of hard-earned success!

Xian is an ongoing human being. Come say hi at xiangoh.com.

.

Made in United States
Troutdale, OR
11/26/2024

25352723R00120